FROM THE
GUTTER-MOST
TO THE
UTTER-MOST

VIVIAN TALBOT

Vivian Talbot
vwtalbot@yahoo.com

Cover design, formatting, and layout done by Michael Talbot.

Print ISBN: 979-8-9910988-0-9

INTRODUCTION

The content of this book might be a little disappointing to some. The thing is that a lot of people are fascinated with the drama and excitement in *My Story*. Unfortunately, this book is NOT about my story, as some would have it, but about God's love manifested in the life of someone who dared to trust Him. Someone who, under normal circumstances, you would be glad to assist in crucifying because of the lifestyle he was living. However, God imposed Himself in his life to show the world that He God, "rules in the affairs of men," and if we would dare to allow Him, we can have the experiences we so yearn for. In reading this book, you will be troubled, and you will question its validity and authenticity. Can these things really be true? Could someone have such a relationship with God? It will trouble you, on one hand, if you are comfortable in your lifestyle and situations— and on the other hand, it will bring comfort to your relationship with God. No longer will you be burdened with trying to "find" God in your circumstances; rather, you will have full confidence in His Word, that He "will never leave you nor forsake you." You will know that you can never be too far away to be out of His reach because, "even if you make your bed in hell there shall His Hand find you."

Life is slipping by a lot of us, but we are powerless to do anything about it. Stop! Read this book, and trust God to give your life a make-over. I want us to know this fact: when the Lord made us He gave us free will. If we are true to ourselves and honest enough to admit it, that anytime we find ourselves in some kind of trouble or mess, it is usually due to us utilizing our freewill under the guise of intelligence or making some kind of "intelligent decision." Nothing is wrong with intelligence. Pause and check it out. Whenever the use of our freewill gets us into some forms of trouble, we look for a way to manage it, right? We talk about *God's Perfect Will* all the time and the Scriptures are saturated with instances of it being seen and proven, and we seem to live it. But, the question and baffling thing is: *Why don't we ask the Lord for a swap of Will?* Why not have His perfect will for your will, since it always gets you into trouble, anyway? We should say, "Lord, thank you for giving me this freewill, but I am having a problem with it. Every time that I get myself in trouble and sin against You, I can trace it back to me using my free will. So, please Lord, can we have a swap of our wills? Take back my freewill and give me your Will. That way, I can't go against Your Will anymore, because it will guide me. Your Will, Lord for my will."

If we do that, I guarantee that our life will be a whole lot better than what it is now. This is not to say that everything is going to be perfect instantly and automatically. Mistakes are still bound to occur because we will still have to get accustomed to and under- standing God's Will. It's a daily process. But, I dare you to try it. In life, when someone who is above us asks us to do something, we should question him or her, as the saying goes, "when he says jump, you should respond, 'how high?'" But, when you are under God's Will, you are not supposed to ask how high when He asks you to jump. You just jump as high as you can because you trust Him. That way you never question God or His authority. You just do what He requires of you. In essence, you have now become God's robot doing whatever He desires of you. Truth be told, this robot concept is very hard to accept. But, isn't it the best way to live if our desire is to please God? We find it difficult to submit to God's will, but the most surprising thing is we allow many people and situations to hold us hostage, use and manipulate us. How is it that we can easily submit to people who are not perfect, who are as weak as we are and who, in most cases, do not wish us well, instead of God? Why don't we let God do it; the only One that we are all certain of that will not abuse or mistreat us. Let us give it a try.

Another thing I would like to point out is that this book is not going to be a sequel, or a chronology because, once again, it is not a story of my life; it is an highlight of a set of events where God has chosen to show Himself strong. So read and allow God to speak to you and use you.

Vivian Talbot; circa 1975
The "Gutter-most"...

GOD'S LOVE MANIFESTED

The nozzle of the 12-gauge Remington repeater shotgun was just about 6 inches from my face, with the business-end pointing towards the windscreen of the car, as it exploded, again and again in rapid succession. The windshield of the taxi I was driving shattered in a thousand pieces, as the other two shotguns joined in the foray. By this, *Ruller*, in the backseat behind me, started to reload. *Ras*, the other backseat occupant, and *Serpent* in the front passenger seat were still going at it when I got a breather from Ruller's barrage which left the left side of my face numbed. The police car in front of us was disintegrating very fast, as it took some real punishment from the three shotguns. It was almost impossible for me to do anything after I ducked down. At one point I tried to rise only to have my head almost blown off when Ruller was firing.

The first volley from us took about a minute and a half while the police were not able to let off a single round. A sudden eerie silence descended in the air and things suddenly seemed strange. The shotguns were silent inside the car and were starting to go off outside. I looked, and only to discover that Serpent was not in the seat beside me. His door was open. And that was when the reality suddenly dawned on me: *I was alone in the car*. The other guys had left. As I swiveled to get out too, I found my legs tied up in the taxi radio cable. And that was when all hell broke loose, again. The police had recovered from the initial shock and ferocity of our firing and started to return the fire. In addition, some other patrol cars seemed to have appeared out of nowhere, and they were certainly pouring it on. This must have been a trap. There was no way so many cops could have got to the site so quickly. The number of explosions beating in the taxi was like hell had opened. The explosions were so much, that it was as if they were just one long roar of bellows. I could hear the projectiles whistling around, hitting the sides of the car, the dashboard, and the seats. They were coming on, relentlessly.

The police, by this, had realized that they had me trapped. There was no escape. Gunshots had closed the open passenger door. I was trying to make myself as small as possible. The projectiles were getting close. The dashboard had become total scrap and splinter. The door handle just disintegrated as I looked up to try to open it. This was when reality hit home. I was trapped. I would be riddled like a sieve if I even try to raise my head. I snuggled down in the cavity under the steering wheel. I fit in there quite easily because I was very small, about 5ft, and just over 100lbs. I could barely see over the steering wheel when sitting in the driver's seat.

It was then that I saw it: a face, a very dark and evil. It seemed solid, like it could be touched, but at the same time, I could see right through it as if it was made of smoke. Was it my imagination? No, not at all. It was as real as the control pedals (gas, clutch, and brake) of the car in front of me. It was right there in front of me, floating in space. It was there for me. And it smiled. As it smiled my entire body went into a shiver. It's as if I was dipped into a drum of ice. And without knowing I knew what it was. It was *Death*. Death had come to visit me. My time had come.

Three weeks earlier, five of my friends died in an ambush in *Linstead*. They had gone to rob the bank, and, on the way back, they were all ambushed, and killed in the car. And here I was, trapped and visited by Mr. Death himself. I came back to reality from memory lane when a bullet whizzed through my locks. I looked at Mr. Death and said,

"Mi nuh ready yet. (*I am not ready yet.*)"

I was not going to die. Suddenly, something came over me. Call it a feeling, a mood, whatever. Don't ask me what. I don't know; even after decades I just cannot explain it. The sound of gunfire did not seem real anymore. I seemed to have lost track of reality and the danger that surrounded me. Something or someone had come over me and there didn't seem to be any care in the world anymore. It's as if I was getting out of bed from a very peaceful night's sleep. So, I just got up and walked out of the car. Yes, I walked right out of the car, past the officers who were still shooting at the car and went about fifty feet down the dirty lane. I jumped over the fence on my right, through a yard, backed up the parallel lane, and walked behind the police, who were still shooting at the car. I crossed the road and went up into the hills.

The shootout took place on the road running parallel to the hill at the base, east to west. This was an inner-city area with zinc fences on both sides of the road. The first lane I went down was about 6ft wide and the dirt surface was hardened by the thousands of feet trekking it daily. Sitting on the hill I could see the police still pounding the taxi with gunshots. Perplexed, I sat down to watch the outcome. The shooting finally stopped, and an eerie silence descended on the area. There was no one visible. They all ran for cover, and the dogs were unusually silent. In fact, the entire area was still and quiet. It all seemed so unreal: the board houses, the dirt road, the empty roads, the police still squatting behind their cars. Is this a picture from a movie or something? Then suddenly, the voice of a policeman brought me back to reality,

"Di bwoy mus dead. Go draw out di body! (*The boy must be dead. Go and pull out his body!*)"

An officer stirred and started to approach the car, crouched with pistol extended. He was not taking any chances. As he reached the side of the car, he stuck his gun in and fired a couple of rounds. He grabbed the door and yanked it open, gun still extended. Then he stood up straight and shouted,

"No one nuh in deh! (*There is no one in there!*)"

The long string of expletives which followed reflected the disbelief, anger, and fear the officers were experiencing. How could this be?

I was suddenly brought back to the stark reality of what was happening. I started sweating, my knees got weak, my stomach tightened, my head hurt and my ears were ringing like hell. The left side of my face was raw and tender from the powder burns received from being too close to the business end of a shotgun. Then, I thought, "*I got to get the hell out of here.*" And I took off through the hills for home.

- - - -

When I woke up that morning, there were great expectations for what was supposed to happen. That day was a great promise for a lot of us. This was supposed to be our biggest hit yet. For weeks this was being planned and was supposed to be a "*piece of cake.*" The bank we were going to rob was sitting all by itself and currently holding a lot of extra cash to handle the payroll of two very big companies, each of which had a very large work force. So, this was going to be good for us; the largest we would have ever taken. But, I should have known that things would not be alright. All the signs of the unexpected were there. I woke up late, and unlike me, could not find the other guys; my belly had this queasy feeling. But, I ignored it all.

At about 8.30, I went to *Rockfort* to find the other guys waiting for me. Most naturally Ruller was upset. He doesn't like to be late.

He hates it— so I got to watch my back. He can't be trusted. He has no friends. We all tolerated him because of his usefulness. He is cold and heartless and kills at the drop of a hat. No matter who you are, he's not someone to mess with. And he's got guns, lots of them. He was about seventeen years old, just over five feet, and lived with his grandmother. His parents were abroad. So, from a very early age, he was on his own, like the rest of us. Parents or not, we were on our own. Serpent was the tallest and the joker in the pack. He too was from Rockfort. Ras was the only *out-a-port* man. He and I were the smallest, and man, he was serious. I must have heard him speak twice, but he and Ruller were tight. He too would kill you at the drop of a hat, without hesitation.

As we gathered to go over the final plans at Ruller's grandmother's backyard, Serpent— with a gun stuck in his waist fully exposed— ticked off Ruller. We were able to get it under control and started to move out to go get a car. I was to be the driver. We walked up to the hillside where we removed the shotguns from their hiding place, loaded them and headed to the house of the taxi we earmarked to use. We knocked on the owner's door and woke him up. He had worked all night and was still very groggy when he came to the door. He almost fainted when he saw these four juveniles pointing shotguns at him. He thought we were there to rob him of his cash and started crying saying,

"I gave it all to my baby's mother before I came home this morning!"
"We no want you money. Jus gi mi di car keys, (*We do not want your money. Just give me the car keys,*)" Ruller said. He turned to fetch them, and I followed him into the house and took them from him. "Nuh worry u self wi a go tek good care of it. And if u keep u mouth shut u might even smile when wi cum back. But if u do not keep u mouth shut then u baby mother a go duh nuff bawlin (*Don't worry. We are going to take good care of it. And if you keep your mouth shut, you might even smile when we come back. But, if*

9

you do not keep your mouth shut, then your baby's mother will go down). You understand?"

With a nod, he indicated that he would comply with us.

We all got into the Yellow Cab and drove off down the hill. I took the road that ran along the foot of the *Wareika Hills,* passed the limestone quarry and the old pump house, and over into Back Bush. The people we passed must have been wondering what was going on because the driver could not be seen. I was too short and had to be looking through the steering wheel. All four of us were under twenty and very small in stature. Ruller and the guys were arguing all along the way about the way they were carrying the shotguns. They were holding them like soldiers sitting in an army truck. Everyone we passed could see them sticking up in the air.

When we reached Back Bush and hit the street, about 70 yards long, the place was deserted. Thinking back now, that was very strange. Someone is always on the street side or the corner. This is the nature of the Inner-city. It is never a lonely place. There is always some-one around, especially at this hour of the morning. About halfway down this piece of street, a police car came around the corner driving very slowly. I slowed down too as I heard the guys cranking up the shotguns.

"Yow, a just one car dis. A no nutten. Hide di dawg dem an mek him pass (*It is just one car. It's nothing. Hide the guns and let him pass*)," I whispered. But, before I realized what was happening the police swung over and slammed into my car head-on. It was then that all hell broke loose.

- - - -

My mom had a hard time taking care of the ten of us. She had one room and we had to sleep head to toe for as many of us as possible to fit on the panel bed. When she woke up to go to work every morning, none of us were ever awake then. She had to leave very early to get to Vineyard Town and to the house where she did domestic work. She had to get there early to prepare breakfast for the family, so that they could get to go to work. And the worst part is that she had to walk from Wareika Hills to get there. There were no buses running on that route. So, after walking about five miles to get there, she would spend the entire day doing housework, on her feet. She would prepare dinner, and stay until they got home and ate. Then, she would clean up after them before she walked the five miles back home to us, at about ten at night. Most of us would have been asleep by then. How we managed through the day was very ad hoc. Most of the details are very vague right now. I remember a few times her waking us up to give us something to eat. When leaving in the morning, she would leave some stuff for us with the bigger ones in charge. But unfortunately, it was never enough. During the day, it was every man for himself. The bigger ones moved all over the place with their friends, and before long we all got friends to hang out with. We all had to learn how to survive, and we learned fast. By age nine or ten, we all were able to do a good job at cooking— Mom made sure of that when she had her days off, which was few and far between as far as I can remember. And hustling was the order of the day. There was no shortage of tutors because the community was full of kids with similar lifestyles. Running the streets and going to the seaside was the routine. On the streets, anything that was easy pickings and could be sold would provide earnings and at the sea, we would dive for conk and help to dive up fish when the fishermen use dynamites.

For me, it was lonely and frustrating, especially when one of my friends talked about the things he would do with his father.

"Daddy said this..."
"Daddy said that...."
"I am going to tell my father..."
"Daddy took me to this place or that place..."

It was very depressing. So, I kept changing my friends and started hanging out with some others who did not talk so much about their fathers. There was an emptiness and a longing. Without even being able to explain it then I knew that my life was missing something very important. When I went home, there was no one there to talk to. I mean, *really talk to*; no one to tell me about things like the other kids. No one I could ask questions. No one I could look up to. My bigger brothers were never there, and I guess that they too were having similar problems. As for mom, she also needed someone on whom to lean. It was obvious in the expressions on her face. Seeing that hurt. I could see her expressions go off in the distance some-times, and this helped to drive me away from home to seek peace for myself, because it seemed to be every man for himself.

When it was time for school Mom was not able to monitor us. Being out for up to eighteen hours of the day most times, she could barely put food in our bellies. She tried her best, but it was a losing battle for her. To help ease the stress on her she sent me to live with an elderly couple in the country. They sent me to school at first, but could not manage and had to return me to my mom when I was about eleven years old. By twelve/thirteen, I was officially out of school. I just quit. Schoolwork was too overwhelming, and I just could not grasp or retain anything. I remember going to class for two or three days over two weeks. Then, it dropped to two or three times a month. However, what finally pushed me out was when my class teacher asked us to answer the questions she set on the board. Everyone except me was able to answer them. I was never able to do or turn in any homework. And that was very embarrassing.

So, I just quit.

Without anyone monitoring me, I just did what I wanted to do, and that was 'running the streets.' There were more than enough friends around to choose from, and lots of places to go hang out. So, I started hanging out with the bigger guys and *moving* with them, learning how to *do the thing*. You see, Wareika Hills is a haven of learning. Guys from all over the city would come there and just hang out and we the younger ones would sit and listen to their stories. Before long I was engulfed in the lifestyle. Then, there were the *Dreads*. These men would sit and talk to you for hours and hours about *livity*, about consciousness, about the system, about Babylon. They seemed to know everything about everything and before long I was sold out to *the cause*.

"Babylon must fall, an all informer mus dead! (*Babylon must fall. And informants must die!*)" In this, I had found a purpose. My purpose was to fight the system and at age thirteen I was full-time, very feared, and *very* deadly.

At thirteen I was very small in size, weighing about a 100lbs and just about five feet, hence I got the name *Little Thirteen*. Pretty soon, because of my fearlessness, my name started going around and the police got wind of it. As my name began to be linked with several incidents, robberies, shootings, and murders, most of which I had no clue about, I became a man of great interest to them and they came looking for me, without success. You see, the name was well known, but the face was a mystery. Not many people knew who I was. This was when I started to drop a lot of my friends, or they dropped me because I was becoming "too hot." I was a full-blown *WANTED* man. Poor Mom, she didn't have a clue of what was going on. Even my bigger brothers were not aware of my true activities until I hit 'the list' and the police started hunting me. You see, I did most of my activities outside of my community. I learned from the Dreads that, "a bird doesn't mess in his own nest". So, I kept my nest clean, and the Hills was my sanctuary.

- - - -

Wareika Hills is in the Southeastern section of the mountain range that runs along the center of the Island, east to west. There is the Blue Mountain Range in the east and the Cockpit Range in the west. Wareika is the southernmost section of the Blue Mountain Range. It runs from Harbor View in the east, to Beverly Hills in the northwest, with Windward Road in the south running east to west, and Mountain View Avenue running south to north. Its true direction is east-south-east to west north-west with Harbor View, Rockfort, Norman Gardens, Jessie City, Back Bush, Top Range, and Beverly Hills being the main Communities along the 'seaward' side. Jessie City and Back Bush were originally called Wareika Hills, while I was growing up, and was the main area where my friends and I hung out.

The hills are a carpet of green with most of the foliage not higher than about ten feet and very thorny. However, there were a lot of sweetsop trees, lots and lots of birds– especially the different types of doves. There was also the occasional wild pig which we shot at for fun (*wi fire-bun di trenton*).

This place provided a haven for four types of people. First, there were the refugees; those from the country who wanted to find somewhere in town, a part of the so-called "*Urban drift;*" and the second later set started in the late 60's and early 70's. These were the ones fleeing from another community because of the political tribalism that had flared up in the West. The type of political tribalism seen in the West did not come to this area until about 1974, so it was like a haven and a place where one could put down some roots. Then thirdly, there were the Dreads, who wanted to stay close to nature and at the same time

14

have quick and easy access to the city. They could be seen coming and going in the Hills every day, and right at the border of the bushes and the houses and zinc fences would be a point of congregation for them. As kids, we would go hang out with them and listen to their stories/counsel. I used to love this part. They had a lot to say about everyone and everything, eating habits, nature, God, people, Government, the *system*, Babylon, foreign affairs, history, slavery, Africa, growing up, how to be strong, the importance of being a man, dress code (male and female). And they were very, *very* convincing too. Most of these talks took place around the chalice (*ganja pipe*). It was very interesting to hear the pipe being blessed. This was where I learned my first Bible quotations. And this was my first university. I was finally getting some questions answered. I finally found something to belong to. A lot of the mysteries of life did not seem so mysterious after all. I had something to look forward to.

Fourthly, there were the *Steppers* and *Hot Steppers*. Steppers were men and women who were involved in criminal activities. They were not necessarily wanted, but were involved and some were school and working folks. While Hot Steppers were men and women who were outright wanted. These were those who were on the run and were always in shootouts with the police. A point of note here is, society makes it to seem as if men are the only perpetrators of crime and criminal activities, but you would be very surprised to know the number of women that are robbing, shooting, and killing people. That is why some men will not hesitate to shoot, maim, or kill a woman because they know that she will not hesitate to put them down.

By virtue of the fact that the East was not experiencing the politics of the West and tribalism of the South, people were flocking to the East for safety . They knew that if they happened to encounter someone they had some beef or conflict with, there would be no violence because it was not allowed in the East or the Hills. The East was a neutral ground, and no one was allowed to violate that, no matter who you were or where you came from. You would either die or be banned if you violated the law. Also, the guys from the East or the Hills were welcomed everywhere because we did not take sides. That was before politics came.

Because of the adventures of the Hot Steppers and the radical approach to life by the Dreads, my life became a hybrid version or a combination of both lifestyles. And before I knew it, I was a gun-toting dread. The no-nonsense approach to life served me well as a Stepper. Thus, I believed in having many *Queens*, but never abusing or hitting any one of them. The "*Haves*" became my target because they represented the oppressor of the poor. I despised the "*Church*" because they were the "*Arm of Babylon*" who came to us with the Bible in one hand and took our riches with the other. The "*Informer*" was the scourge of the earth because they were selling their own to the enemy, just like they did Marcus Garvey. The Police were the other Arm of Babylon that needed to be chopped off. The non-violent approach to life of the Dreads was not for me, and running away from the police with your back to them by the Steppers and Hot Steppers was not for me either. Thus, I took the most aggressive view and habit from both the Dreads and the Steppers and molded my own philosophy. I would take what I can get and never die running away from the police. So, *Rasta* was my god, *the gun* my protector, and *the weed* was the sacrament of peace to my tortured soul; *and vengeance was mine.*

At times, life became very complicated and risky. As I grew up my fame grew also and with that came the attention of the police and the reduction of the number of friends who would "*walk*" with me; the few who did would be as crazy and as dangerous as I was, or even worse. I started doing things that were thought to be just outright mad. One night, a couple of us wanted to go to a dance out of town, so we needed a car. We saw some cars parked at a party and I decided to take one. While I was inside bridging the wires, I suddenly felt a presence and looked up only to see dozens of faces looking at me in the car. They pulled me out and the mob descended on me like a swarm of vultures on dead meat. Within minutes I lost track of the blows that I was getting. I was numbed. The only thing I was aware of was being bounced from place to place as each blow connected. I was also aware of this person wanting to cut my ears off. He was saying that he wanted it to be a sign and lesson to me that I should never steal again. Somehow, I lost track of how long this went on, but the police came, and I was handed over to them. And thank God he never did get that chance to cut my ears off. I ended up with some fractures and a few broken ribs, but was never taken to the hospital.

After a few days, I was given bail after being charged with attempting to drive away a car without the owner's consent. This was very neat because they never had a clue of who they had in custody. None of them knew my face or my real name. And before word could reach them, I was out on bail. However, the police made a mess of the case by sending me and the files to separate courts. My first time in jail was at age nineteen. I did not pay much attention to trying to sort out the case. I just did not care. No way was I going to put myself at the mercy of the "*Shitstim*" (System). Because I was sure that by this, they must have heard that they made a very serious blunder in letting me go. The truth of this was made obvious when I was arrested the second time. It is said that once you go to jail it will follow you no matter what you do, or don't do. And that seems to be so true. Anyway, life continued on its merry way.

The life of a wanted man has some very strange perks to it, some of the best girls wanted to be with me without question, money would come without question, respect and fear came without question, and nobody spoke tough to you at all. There was also the other side of that where life would become lonely, depressing, and very stressful and most friends would no longer want to be seen with you. There was nowhere safe to sleep. You'd never know when a *friend* would call the police on you, and even the very person you were walking with might kill you at any moment. You were safe nowhere.

Life was one big and very complicated trauma. Each day passed by without meaning or purpose. The reality had now set in that what I thought was my purpose in life had left me out in the cold. I had graduated and was out on my own. There was no longer any sitting down and reasoning with the Dreads. I was too hot, and they wanted nothing to do with me. And the nest that I would rest in no longer provided that haven that it was supposed to have provided. Each night I wondered where I would get to lay my head and hoped that I would not have to sleep. When I get up in the morning, I must be sure no one sees me coming out of my *hole* because I might just have to go back there sometime in the future. Bob Marley's song, "*Cold Ground Was My Bed Last Night, and Rock Stone Was My Pillow*" took on new meaning for me and very aptly described most of my sleeping arrangements; cellars, roofs, trees, or just about anywhere that offered privacy and kept me out of sight. I never slept at the same place as the other guys. I just never trusted anyone that much. Food for the day most times was no problem. Money was usually around and if not, we would ask a friend to "*run a boat*." However, sometimes, we needed to run and leave the boat before it "*lands*" because "*the place got hot*". Gradually, I became a loner because most of the other guys usually got themselves in situations that attracted a lot of attention. So, they just kept dying or going to jail one by one, and I was not going to go like that.

- - - -

Looking back now I realize that God was watching over me.

"WHAT?! God watching over a gunman?!"

Yes! A resounding *YES!!!* The many escapades I have been through and the way they happened make me know now– beyond the shadow of a doubt– that God was *divinely* protecting me; not in my sins, or the committing of sins, but that my life would be spared for me to come into *His Purpose*. I would be at places with the other guys a lot of times and would just have a feeling to move, which I always did. Then, within minutes, the place would be raided by the police looking for us. Situations like that most times ended up in shootouts, including death and injury. Escapades like these only helped to increase my reputation, especially among my peers. On several occasions, they would ask me about the *obeahman* (*charm*) my Mon was using to protect me and why I was so protected. Pretty soon, I was the only one among us who was never shot or wounded, and up until the car incident I was never caught or jailed. With all that, I kept glorying in the fact that I was so skillful and *slippery*.

I started to pay fewer and fewer visits to my home. So, one morning after I slept on the roof of a concrete structure down by the beach, I decided to get some fresh clothes. On my way up Mountain View Avenue, I was walking as if I owned the world and was a free man. However, that world was going to come crashing down soon. My senses had become so dull with self-confidence or something and I was very unaware of my surroundings, which was extremely unlike me. I had mastered the art of observation and reading people's actions and it was very unlikely to catch me off-guard. However, I was not aware of the two young men who were walking towards me until they grabbed me. Everything said that I should have noticed them. Their mode of dressing was wrong. They were properly dressed in slacks and long-sleeved shirts with ties like they worked in some kind of office. At this time of the day, about ten in the morning, normally no one like that should be in the vicinity, the Jacques Road area. I also did not have a gun on me, another unusual situation.

This morning I suffered the indignity and humiliation of walking on the street with these two young cops, for about two miles from Mountain View and the bottom of Jacques Road to the Vineyard Town Police Station. To my surprise, when I asked them why they were arresting me, they said that I absconded the court charges made against me, in which the officer made a mix-up of sending the case to the wrong court. And no matter how hard I tried to explain to them about the mix-up, they would not listen. I had to wait until the officer in charge of the case came. This was good, but also not good. It was good that they did not know who I was. And I hoped it stayed that way. It was not good because I would not like for anyone who knew me to come to the station and see me. My greatest fear was someone who knew my identity seeing us and telling them who I was. I experienced my worst fear— because that was exactly what happened.

About twenty minutes after being taken to the station a carload of detectives drove into the station. It was obvious that they came for business judging from the way they sped into the station yard and jumped out of the car. They rushed into the Station house and hastily asked the Station Guard where Little Thirteen was. On hearing this, my whole world crumbled. At the time, I was still handcuffed to the bench I was sitting on. There was a lot of confusion everywhere. These detectives were from the HQ at Elletson Road and Little Thirteen was one of their priorities. Their motto was that *you don't bring in someone like me. I must die.* So, they were in a total rage against the two Rookies who brought me in alive. After much argument and debate they took the cuffs off me and walked back out of the Guard Room. I could see a couple of them peeping from the back room and another two were crouching outside under the window. I saw a gun on the desk unprotected. They deliberately left the empty gun there with the hope that I would grab it and try to make a run so that they could shoot me down. And the gun would be the evidence against me.

With the failure of this trap, they took me to the HQ at Elletson Road for interrogation— and this went with much vigor and ferocity. I lost track of how long it went on for. They were not trying to get information per se, but rather inflicting punishment on me. It was vengeance because they did not get to kill me. Imagine being beaten with a 25lb station house logbook on your head and across your back, spread-eagle across a desk, with your legs cuffed on one side and your locks tied to the legs of the desk on the other side. When they are done you are unable to stand or even hold up your head. When they had their fill and were fully tired, they took me to the Central Lock-up to face identification parade.

A few days later, they came for me from the cell for the ID Parade. This was my first experience and was not aware of how they *cook up.* During the *interrogation* at Elletson Road they had taken a picture of me that I wasn't aware of, but I was about to find out. The detective in charge of the parade made me to stand in position #3, and warned me, "Don't move." The minute he left a friend of mine who was also in jail and was put on the Parade immediately rushed to me and told me to move to his position #9. I just didn't understand and hesitated. He grabbed me and said, "Di Parade cook, move! (*The Parade is rigged. Move!*)" Still not understanding, I obeyed and went to position #9. Seconds later, a gentleman came in and went straight to position #3, stuck his finger in the guy's chest and said, "this is the man, this is the man!" That was when I knew what a *"cooked parade"* was. The detective had shown the witness the picture he had taken of me and told him the position I was standing in. That was why when he came in, he went straight to position #3. Nevertheless, he still messed up because he did not bother to look at the face. He was so sure of the number.

When the detectives realized what happened, they were *pissed*, to say the least. So, they decided not to take any more chances and charged me only for the shooting that took place in Back Bush, and later transferred me to GP (*General Penitentiary*), where I was remanded in custody for trial. While at GP I was a loner; most of the people I knew did not pay much attention to me (we weren't that close anyway). During the trial at the Home Circuit Court, I stood for my own defense. Poor Mom... she took it hard and could not afford an attorney. And quite naturally I was sentenced to 56 years in prison. The moment felt like something unreal. When I was taken back to GP to my 5x8 cell and the door was slammed behind me, it was like entering a time warp. The other two guys in the cell were trying to get me to talk about how the trial went but I was zoned out.

I can't remember if I slept at all that night. When I was let out of the cell in the morning I was like a zombie, just going through the motions. The next few days just flowed into each other. But then, my sister came to visit me, and naturally, there was nothing much to talk about, except about Mom, who had become an emotional wreck. Life in prison was nothing I expected– then again I didn't know what to expect. I was just living my life with no thought of consequences. As the days wore on and reality set in, I became more bitter and vengeful; I guess not because I got caught– that was my own fault for dropping my guard. I was angry because of the condition I was caged up in, like an animal.

A few weeks in I received a visit from a lawyer who was going to represent me for an appeal. This was a joyous moment. There was light at the end of the tunnel. The only subjects of discussion going on were appeals, lawyers, and visitors. And my lawyer was one of the best at representing appeals, and that gave me much hope. The only thing I had to be worried about was how long it was going to take. There were guys there whose appeal was pending for like two and three years. Regardless, it was very comforting to know that I had this lawyer on my case. There was always an air of great anticipation when one of the guys got a visit from his lawyer. 'The Freedom Light' would seem to be shining much brighter and everyone shared in the charged atmosphere. If the news is that someone lost the appeal, then gloom would descend like a wet dirty blanket over the entire cell block. Those of us who still had cases pending would pray to whomever/whatever we pray to and hope that we would not share in the wet blanket.

Five months later, it would be my turn to hear from my lawyer. However, the worst part is when the appeals are decided, and your lawyer does not come to give you the result himself, but only sends the document to the prison because he doesn't want to face you due to the disappointment. And this is usually after *lock-down* (after 3pm). So, to be in your cell at that hour and hear your name causes a choking effect. So, when I heard my name, I immediately felt like I was having diarrhea; my head started swimming, and my knees got very weak. The look on the faces of the other guys in the cell did not help at all. All the signs were dismal. Only five months? Why didn't the lawyer say something? Why didn't he come himself? I heard the Warders opening the cell. There was my letter of condemnation. He handed me the sheet of legal paper and said, "You are going home!!!" That was when I thought that I did in fact *mess* myself. All I could do was scream. With that, the cell block realized what had happened and erupted.

I had won my appeal.

"Mi bus di case! (*I won the case!*)"
56 years in prison.
"*Conviction Quashed and Sentence Set Aside*" – the legal expression used for the occasion, I believe.

- - - -

How I got home and the events of the next two or three weeks, right now are very vague in my mind. But one thing I knew was that my life became different; not different in a good way but hardened and more fearless and determined. I could still smell the result of 16 months spent in that 5x8 cage/hole and the times I had to hide my face and wrap it in a towel because one of the other guys wanted to *use his bucket*.

For me, it was not back to life as usual. Everything had stepped up a few notches. Quite a few of the guys were either killed or in jail, and those still around had stepped up their game. Things just had to be different. In my 16 months, I had matured quite a bit and I vowed that I would not go to jail like that anymore. I easily slipped into my routine with a new fervor. And I realized that the ugly head of politics was creeping into the community. That was not for me. So, little by little I had to start my own thing. People were noticing that I was not very much into what was going on. I was spending a lot of time outside the community trying to find a new enclave. I was meeting with a few guys who respected me and were willing to follow me. Bournemouth Gardens was such a place. It was not an inner-city; there was a beach, and a community swimming pool, and none of the guys there had any guns. I had to build this from scratch; get guns for them, teach them how to hustle and make money, and look out for each other. So, my time was taken up between Bournemouth and Bull Bay.

By this time, I had connected with an old friend who was in Bull Bay. I started to visit and strengthen his hand there, which played well for him. And I didn't mind because he gave me a house that I could stay in without a problem. So effectively, we were both "running the area." Things were going very peachy; but not for long. When things are going too nice, be careful... Be *very* careful.

Then, two incidents of note took place that stirred up my nest. While we were there organizing the area, the most dangerous cop at the time was sent out there to clean up the area. So, tonight, me and my three "soldiers" were down by the beach road. At about eight in the night, they started prompting me to leave to go over to the Hills where I had a house. I was very reluctant because I was trying to sweet talk this little girl I liked. She was very much into me, so I was not just going to walk away like that until I was sure that I had made the right impression on her. They kept prompting me and I kept refusing until I told them to start walking and I would catch up with them. So, they relented and left. Within two minutes of their leaving, the quietness of the night was thunderously destroyed by a barrage of explosions. Sounded like about thirty or forty shots were fired all at once, which meant that there must have been about fifteen or twenty guns firing. Within about a minute later there was another barrage. This time about twelve to fifteen rounds were fired. Then, there was silence. This was taking place just about a hundred meters from where I was standing. Without knowing, in my heart, I immediately knew what had happened. The guys were ambushed and killed. I took cover in the house hoping that the owners there would not say anything. And there I stayed until everything was over six to eight hours later. The story is, that this detective and his squad were in the dry riverbed waiting for us. They heard about my movements, and they weren't taking any chances. So, when they saw the three guys, they just laid it on them killing everyone. The second set of shots was in the head of the kid who resembled me. He was shot seventeen times in the head. His face was unrecognizable. If it had not been for the fact that I was so bent on "smooching up" to this girl, I would have been there, and that minced-meat face would have been mine.

A few weeks later, about four hundred meters away, across the road up on the hillside I was at a dance. Somehow, I leaned on the sound box and fell asleep— in the dance, standing up, while the music was playing.

Strange? Yes. Weird? Yes. True? Yes.

You see, when God has His hand on you, He can and will do very strange and weird things in your life. Suddenly, something woke me. Confused, I looked and the dance was empty. As I looked towards the gate, I saw some women coming back inside. I stopped one of them and asked her what was happening. She gave me this very strange look and then responded, "Police raid di dance an gone wid all di man dem a jail. (*The police raided the dance. All the men have been taken to jail.*)" The sum of the situation is that this same policeman and his squad raided the dance, took everyone outside to the street, putting the women on one side of the street and the men on the other. After searching all the men, they were all forced to "*drape*" each other in the waist and march single file down the street to the station, which was about five hundred meters away. Incidentally, what woke me up was when the DJ started to play the music again. So, through it all, I was leaning on the sound box fast asleep without a clue of what was happening. The DJ and I were the only males who were not marched to the station that night. I think that I was made invisible just like what happened the morning in the shootout at Back Bush. God was looking out for me, big-time. And soon, my lifestyle was going to catch up with me.

A chain of events was being set in place that would change my life forever. One of my girlfriends had a baby for me and she was having problems with her mother to get me out of her life. Incidentally, I realized that they had moved to Bull Bay near where I was hanging out. My baby's mother's mother warned her that if ever I came to the house, my baby's mother would have to leave immediately. Naturally, that law could not hold. There was no way that my child would be so close, and I would not go to look for her. And I did. And she heard. And true to her word, she took the baby and came looking for me.

When she couldn't find me, she put the baby in the middle of the street and told one of my friends to come and get her. Luckily, my baby's mother found me first with the baby. I was blue with rage and only God knows what I would have done to my baby's mother's mother. Anyway, I took the baby and asked one of the guys to come with me to take the baby to my mom's house in Mountain View. There was a car that we had— it was stolen, naturally— and we headed for Mountain View.

As we hit the main road in Harbor View, we ran into a roadblock. Not wanting to be chased by the police I decided that I would rather go to jail than risk the baby's life. So, I stopped. When the cop came to me by the car window, I tried talking to him to let me go, showing him the baby and explaining what had happened between me, the baby's mother, and her mother. And he agreed to let me go, but I did not have a driver's license, and by this time another cop had come and was listening to what was going on. I asked him to let my friend take the baby home for me, which he gladly accepted. I was then taken to the Harbor View Station. Seeing that all I was going to be charged with was driving without a driver's license, he arranged for me to get Station bail. This meant that I was allowed to go free after signing the bail bond, which did happen.

That was major, because if they had just checked the system or the Bull Bay Station they would have realized that they had made a big catch. Most naturally, I did not go to court and the officer who had arranged my bail was *pissed*. This absence from court was going to be my big downfall, because two weeks later, as I was walking on Windward Road towards Bournemouth; I stepped aside on the sidewalk to let this giant of a man pass me. Before I knew what was happening, he grabbed me lifting me straight off my feet.

I was shocked and confused. This happened right in front of a restaurant.

He took me inside and asked the proprietor to call Elletson Road Station. I kept my cool because I had my gun in my waist. But, this guy was holding my pants waist so tight that I could barely breathe. I was just biding my time hoping that he would loosen up his grip a little. While waiting I started to get very nervous because he wouldn't loosen for one bit, and I had to get to my gun. He picked up on my twisting and squirming and started to search me and found the gun. He shouted about it and the proprietor came out with his gun to help the police. At this point I knew that I was dead. Just about this time a patrol car came for him and saw the activities and they threw me in the back of it. All kinds of thoughts were going through my mind: Going back to prison, the dreaded Gun Court and they had the evidence. I started wondering about the crimes that that gun may have committed, not by me, but by the other guys who may have used it, and what other charges were they going to pin on me. I had to take my chances and try to make a break somehow. However, his one was not going to be easy; they had the evidence, and the judges at Gun Court had the reputation of not going easy on offenders being caught with guns. That was the reason for the Gun Court after all. Gun violence had gotten out of hand and the Government was very desperate about getting it under control.

A few months ago, the sentence in the Gun Court was indefinite detention, but due to an appeal to the Privy Council in England, it was replaced with a mandatory life sentence without the possibility of parole. Legally though, at the time, there was no parole system on the books in Jamaica. You just stay in prison, 20, 30, 40, 50 years in prison based on the sentence handed down by the trial judge and upheld by the appeals Court.

When we reached Elletson Road Station, I was quickly surrounded by detectives who all wanted a piece of me. They took me in a car, along with other cars, and took me to my home to search for more guns. They kept asking me for the other guns, especially the shotguns.

Naturally, they got nothing out of me. They kept examining my pants waist and saw evidence of the constant wear and tear of carrying the gun on the inside of my pants waist. They took them all as evidence. When we got back to the Station the interrogation took on the usual method, beating over the head and back with a 25lb station logbook. I was not taken to one of the jails, as I was hoping but straight to GP. The 4-minute drive was like being locked up in a metal drum and rolled down the hill. When we got out of the car I could hardly stand and was so glad because the beating with the book left me in pain, as they say, "from the crown of my head to the sole of my feet."

Just going through the tunnel into the prison yard brought back dreadful thoughts. One was that I had seen a warder once and chased him down to kill him, but he got away. And warders don't take too kindly to that at all. On my last "visit" I saw them beat a prisoner into uncon-sciousness for a similar matter. Even when he was unconscious, they were still beating him. A senior officer had to intervene. They wanted to kill him.

Oh my God… I was back here at GP in less than *two years*.

- - -

It was evening, and all the cell blocks were locked down. Several of us were being processed because other inmates were brought in from other station jails. I suddenly felt someone grabbing me in the back of my collar and saying, "You remember me?" I turned around and saw the officer I had chased looking down at me. He said, "Yu nuh remember you chase me on Mountain View? Now you inna my place (*Do you remember, you chased me on Mountain View? Now, you are in my place*)!" My whole body became numb. I immediately remembered what happened to the last guy that they accused of that. It was at that point, I knew that I was dead. Dying was not the problem— but the

29

pain being experienced before you die was unbearable. Being beaten with the station logbook was child's-play compared to what was in stock for me. When these guys beat you, calling it *merciless* is a gross understatement. At this point, I was already so weakened from the station logbook experience.

"Put 'im one side. Wi soon deal wid im (*Keep him aside. We will deal with him soon*)," one of them said casually. They intended to finish processing the other inmates and get them out of the way. By this, word had gone around and other officers from the other blocks came by. The number was about 20. Looking back on my life, every incident that had a life and death element in it, there was a miraculous deliverance in there somewhere. Just about when they were ready for me, a senior officer approached us and asked what was going on. He heard about what was about to go down with me, and he stepped in.

This officer was one of my brother's best friends. He was a senior officer, and this was the first time I had met him as a warder. So, he stepped in and took over the case, dispersing them to go back to their posts. Their immediate response to his order showed he was obviously well respected. While they dispersed, there were a few parting threats, which I knew were not idle. I knew that the news would spread to the other officers running the other shifts. The next day was like a living nightmare. I could see the officers coming in and scouting me out. By this, all the other inmates knew that I was marked, and they stayed away from me. I did not move around the block, but stayed right at the door of my cell. One week later, the officers came back for me and again, my *Guardian Angel* stepped in. Both the waiting and uncertainty were killing me– but God had another plan. I can easily say that now because of hindsight. Looking back, I knew that it was God's way of looking out for me.

During my stay at the Gun Court, court schedule was packed. The men were being scooped up by the dozens and cases were being scheduled for up to a year. Within 4 weeks I was taken to court, yet I did not get a chance to make any contacts. Based on the caseload at the court, no case was being tried yet. I was expecting that my case would have to be mentioned and then I would get a few months' remand before trial, but fate had other plans for me. I was brought before the judge. The police showed him the gun, and the judge asked for my plea. He assigned for me a court-appointed lawyer who, at this point, spoke to him a few times, then he said, "You are guilty."

During all of this, I was in a trance. I came to reality when the police came and took me out of the court. I looked at him questioningly and he said, "You heard the judge: two life sentences. Yu a guh dead a prison bwoy. No parole (*You will die in prison boy. No parole*)." I was on my way out of the courthouse when I saw one of my friends coming in.

"This is the lawyer," he said.
"Mi get sentence already (*I've been sentenced already*)," I responded as I was taken to the holding area to be processed and placed in the prison, which was right there within the same compound.

- - -

I spent the next week or so in the holding cell behind the courthouse, swearing and cussing and blaming myself for being so stupid repeatedly. After about a week, a lawyer came to visit me. There was this dryness and lack of enthusiasm; it was as if the world had stopped, and I was in some sort of cocoon. Everything had closed in on me and I could not make sense of anything around me. I was in *Zombieland*. People kept coming and going, but nothing was real. A couple of weeks later, the lawyer came back and that gave me some sense of hope, which was shattered the minute he opened his mouth. He was not going to represent me... I did not hear anything else that he said. My head was exploding and there was no breath left in me. It was as if someone had sucker-punched me. Life was now— REALLY— at a standstill. I did not know how the conversation went or how it ended, but by the end I was back in my cell.

The nightmarish experience with the lawyer was now wearing off a little and reality was gradually setting in when I was transferred to the Remand section where I would be doing my two life sentences. I saw a few guys that I was acquainted with, in person, and some I only knew by reputation. And most naturally, my reputation preceded me. I became the subject of observation by almost everyone— friends, and foes alike.

The Remand Center was nothing like any prison I had heard about or seen in any movie. It was attached to the military camp and was guarded by the military in the sentry boxes and the perimeter fences. Warders manned the internal operations and the day-to-day administration of the inmates. The police were responsible for the day-to-day operation of the courts and the handling of the transfer of inmates from the courthouse to the holding cells. And everything was painted red. The government said they "wanted it to be red because it is dread." That's why the public called it "Red Fence." There was to be only one hour of exercise time and twenty-three hours of lock-down. There were two things here that were a little better than GP: the front of the cells was grilled, so, there was a lot more fresh air and inmates were allowed outside. Still, there was nothing to do; there were over 200 inmates standing outside and staring out into space.

However, some very big changes happened. Someone sued the government over the conditions of the facility and won. The red color had to be removed because it was said to cause blindness and severe mental trauma— that was considered to be excessively cruel and unnecessary punishment. So before long, we were getting three hours of exercise time.

Within a month or so, I was settling into my routine, hanging out with friends. I was still a loner, but, in that place, people tend to get to know others. Someone has got to have your back; you never know what or when someone might go crazy on you when you are not looking. I have seen it a lot.

It was then that I noticed something very strange and unusual. A couple of elderly ladies were coming in and having church services every Sunday. They just stood out there in the sun and sang, read the Bible, preached, and prayed. Not one person paid them any attention at all. Each Sunday they would come back and go through the same routine: sing, read the Bible, preach, and pray, in the sun. We enjoyed the sun. We spent 21 hours locked in a cell, so it was a welcomed change to get out in the sun. But these two ladies had a choice. What on earth did they think that they were doing? Preaching to us? That was the most ridiculous thought I had ever heard. It wasn't even a good *joke*. But they were serious– very, *VERY* serious. During the week I found myself thinking about them a lot. I didn't understand why, but I did. I wasn't listening to what they were saying, but the fact that they would be back, religiously, every week to go through the same routine was saying something to me. I don't know what, but I was witnessing some-thing very powerful taking place right there in front of me and I could not understand it.

I stood there each week and watched them for a full year. They never flinched or paused; come rain or sun shine, they were there in their routine, singing, reading the Bible, preaching, and praying. After a while, I found that I had started to listen to them. I don't know how it happened. I just realized that I was hearing them preach about things in life that I was acquainted with. They were talking about the thoughts

33

I was having in my head, that even I was afraid to admit to myself. And that was scary... very scary. How can this be? How can they know what I was thinking? How can they be talking about my business— and publicly at that?

Then one Sunday, I caught myself looking to see if anyone else was listening, and I was nervous. No. I could not allow these elderly ladies to mess up my life like that. I had to get rid of them. This cannot continue anymore. So, during the week, I brought up the subject of these two ladies. To my surprise, it was as if the guys were itching to talk about them, and I was further shocked at the fact that there were other people there that were having mental problems with them. So, we all started cursing them. I don't often talk much when I want to do something. I suggested that we stoned them the next time they came in. This the guys were very hesitant to do, but my insistence got two of them to agree with me to stone them the next Sunday. Incidentally during the week, the authorities brought in a 30ft caravan for them to have service in. I am not sure how they got it, but some benevolent person/organization donated it. And it was perfect.

The next few days leading up to Sunday were a living torment: headache, backache, diarrhea, lack of appetite, weakness— everything was wrong. I thought of calling it off but couldn't. I got to keep face. I was the one who insisted on doing it, so I couldn't back out now.

Come Sunday morning, the officers were escorting the women to the new location where the caravan was. They were visibly happy and were really praising God for this blessing. We waited until the service started and I got the other two guys; we each got two grapefruit-sized stones and proceeded to perform a "*works.*" I took the lead and went to the window at the side of the caravan. From there I could get an unobstructed view and not miss any throw. All I remembered was when I pulled back my hand with the stone to let it fly; I was so sure,

I couldn't miss it. That was all I remembered. I lost consciousness, not sure of what happened. The next thing I remembered was opening my eyes and hearing myself say, "Amen." And then I was standing at the altar. And the caravan was full of guys.

Please, don't ask me what happened because I don't know. I was told many different versions of what happened but none of them made sense, nor can I verify any of them. One thing I knew was that something very supernatural happened to me, and I cannot explain it. One version grabbed me though: they said that I came into the caravan and sat down. And all throughout the service, I was fidgeting– twisting and turning and trying to get up but at the same time I was holding myself down on the chair. Every time I did that it created a disturbance, and it was very annoying and distracting. How could I be trying to get up but holding myself down on the chair at the same time? As I said, I don't remember any of this. So again, please don't ask me.

Suddenly all the pain and agony I had felt before left me and I felt very light; it was like I could scream and shout and jump and run and kick. It was like I was watching myself going through all this excitement and was amazed at myself in this state. I had never seen anything like this before. One thing for sure was, though– no one had to tell me– that I was *saved*. I had no clue of what that meant, I just knew. Never been to church, never prayed, and knew nothing about what goes on in church or how a Christian should live or behave. But here I am, saved; the first man to be saved inside of Gun Court. This was going to be the biggest talk around town: "Thirteen turned a Christian."

- - -

After the service was over, *Sister Allison* and I were walking with the warder from the caravan and she said to me, "Now that you have committed your life to the Lord, you are going to lose all your friends.

But remember this one thing, let God be your Best Friend." And this she spoke prophetically, because true to her word, I lost all my friends. No one wanted to be associated with a man who "bowed in prison." That was the most disgraceful and derogatory thing to be seen as in prison. You are now an open target. Anyone who needs a "rank" could take you out and no one would lift a finger to help. On the way to my cell, I could feel the stares digging into my body. For the rest of the day, there was an uneasy hush on the cell block. Everyone came to look at me in the cell. I don't know what they expected to see. Maybe they wanted to see if I seemed different. Confusion was setting in. How do I handle this new life? How do I pray? Wait... I just realized that I can't read the Bible. *I can't read at all.* So, what do I do now?

I then remembered what Sister Allison said about God being my Best Friend. So how did this Best Friend thing work? No one was there to give me any answer to the multitude of questions I was having. Here I was again, another stage in my life where I was having a lot of questions and no one to ask for answers. In my mind, my best friend was like my brethren down the cell block who was now ashamed to call me his friend. So, without even thinking about it I asked God if that is how He was. Somehow inside I felt peace. I can't tell you that I heard His voice or anything like that— I just felt peace and I knew that He had answered me. And that was the beginning of my friendship with my new *Friend.* One thing I remembered was that we chatted every day all day long. I didn't have anyone else to talk to anyway.

As the days passed by, I started to get used to this *Best Friend* thing and we started to have fun. I began to learn how to listen to Him and how to develop confidence in my Friend. This was real. This friendship with God thing worked. We talked and had conversations about everything. I was not being distracted by anything. Everybody seemed to leave me alone, or so I thought. They were plotting against me, and this came to my attention one day while having one of my conversations with my

Big Friend. This inmate just walked up to me and said, "Dem a guh kill yu today after open-up (*A guy will kill you today after open-up*)." That was during the afternoon break.

My conversation with the Lord had become so natural and common-place that I could not tell you if when He responded to me it was audible or just in my heart; it was just a knowing and peace that He had just answered me. It was in this frame of mind that I got this information about their plans to kill me. There was no feeling of fear or trepidation. Just knowing that I was having a conversation with the Lord was enough for me. However, there was the reality that I was going to die. Ironically, I had a sense of excitement that I was going to be seeing the Lord soon. And I welcomed the idea. *Death* was no longer that dreadful thing as it was made out to be. The only reality to me then was that I was going to see God today. And I reacted by my instinct. I got my knife and put it in my waist. I went outside where it was said that they were going to kill me, and rested my back against the wall. I was not going to let anyone sneak up behind me, and continued my conversation with God.

As I stood there waiting, I said to the Lord, "You see these guys, Lord, You know they are not as bad as I am, but because I am now serving you they are going to kill me. Anyway, let them come. One thing though Lord, give me the chance to kill at least three of them before they get me." By this time, about 25 of the guys had gathered outside about 20-30 feet in front of me. "Ok Lord, this is it. Three, I want to kill the one in front. I want to stab him in the heart. When I pull the knife out, I want to slash the throat of the one on his right. I know that by this they would have been upon me, but let me get just one more before it's over." There, they were standing as a tight-knit group as if they were all roped together.

I kept watching and kept talking to God while they were there growling at me, "Christian bwoy, mek wi si how yuh God a go save you now" (*Christian boy, let us see how your God will save you now*)!" Strangely, I was having a bit of fun talking to God about how stupid they were to be all standing together like that when the warders could easily see that something was up. I kept talking to God and they kept growling. This continued for about five or so minutes when they started to disperse one by one from the back.

When the last two were left, in parting one of them said, "Yuh get whe today Christian bwoy (*You got away today, Christian boy*)!"
"God, yuh nuh si dem a guh weh? A dat mi a tell Yu, dem a fool. Dem a idiot" (*God, do You see them all leaving? I tell you, they are fools! Idiots*)!" I said to the Lord, and He smiled. And I smiled too. I was kind of having a feeling of slight disappointment. I did want to kill those three guys, just to discipline them. Also, I wanted to see what this place called Heaven was like. Well, I guess that would have to wait for another time.

Looking back now, I wasn't thinking about being stabbed to death. I guess having that conversation with God took my mind off that. Death was never, and is still never an issue with me. Over time, I learned that all death is, is a transition to the afterlife; to hell if you die in your sins, or to be with the Lord if you die living your life with/for God; no pain, just a smooth transition. All the pain you are going to feel, and experience is in this life, trying to navigate the issues and obstacles you will be experiencing while still here on earth. But one thing I found out, over time, is that there is more pain in anticipating the pain than in ex-periencing the pain itself. If my experience with God in the last couple of weeks is anything to go by, then this is where I am going to spend the rest of my life, having a good conversation with my Best Friend.

It is now with hindsight that I realized what was happening. God had been watching over me all this time and I never had a clue about it. Every time that I found myself in a sure-death situation, I would walk away unscathed, untouched, and I would selfishly claim the glory for myself ascribing the victory to my skill and fearlessness. But I know for sure now that it was God Himself who was intervening in my life for a purpose.

I remember Mom told me of her experience when she was pregnant with me. She was hospitalized several times until they took me out at seven months. I spent the next three months in the ICU. I later spent the next few years in and out of the hospital. I was a late starter and was always behind everyone in life activities. I was never very active and avoided the regular kid's games, especially contact games. I hated to be hit or bounced on. I hated excitement and argument, so I was always on the sideline looking on, not having any real friends at all. I was always thinking about one thing or the other, always trying to figure out life. When I learned of Jeremiah 1:5 ("*Before I formed thee in the belly, I knew thee; and before thou came forth out of the womb I sanctified thee, and I ordained thee a prophet unto the nations*"), I took hold of it and claimed it for myself. And this sure-death experience I just encountered was no exception.

That evening after lockdown, the same three guys that I was hoping to kill came to visit me at my cell. We had the most unusual conversation. They wanted to know who I was talking to while we were outside. "God," I answered simply.
"Then God knew that we were going to kill you and was there just chatting with you?" they asked, obviously very baffled.
"Well, I am not dead," I responded casually.
"Well, I would like to know that God," one of them said as they walked away, still confused. I did not know how else to respond, but I guess that God was satisfied with them seeing His Power being demonstrated, because a few weeks later revival broke out and over a few weeks about twenty guys committed their lives to the Lord.

Sister Allison was ecstatic. After almost two years she finally started to see the work bearing fruit. This, however, brought her a new set of problems. I, for one, was not satisfied with the once-per-week, one-hour service. She could not provide counseling or encouragement because the system would not allow it. Also, they were not prepared to have a bunch of criminals turned religious fanatics on their hands. It was then that I found out that the Penal System actually had a Chaplain. Suddenly he was showing a lot of interest. No one had ever seen him before but now he was there and wanting to meet with us. I was somehow still wary of Christians. I loved and respected Sister Allison, because she was different.

When we went to meet him, he had a lot of accolades for us and how he was so proud that we had taken such a significant step in life. I was not interested in what he was saying anymore and without realizing it, I just tuned him out. I was no longer hearing God through him like I used to— like when Sister Allison was preaching. When he said that he was going to set up a meeting to have all of us confirmed in his church, I reacted. Something sounded very off about that. I was already confirmed by God, so why would I need someone else to confirm me. Sister Allison never said anything to us about any so-called confirmation. He singled out each individual for a reaction/response and each one looked at me for some kind of confirmation. Then he turned to me, and I asked him to let us all discuss it because we all felt committed to Sister Allison. So, he left to return the next week.

Back at the cell block, we had a very extensive debate. The consensus was that even though this guy represented the system and was at its mercy, we were not going to give up Sister Allison. Our loyalty was with her. She was the one who preached to us, and she was the one who prayed over us. She was the one we had been seeing week after week over the years. She was the one who we could always turn to.

Over all those years we weren't even aware of his existence; now he wanted to take us away from Sister Allison. And I was not going to jump ship for this guy who was not even talking to God. We wanted to have more services and Sister Allison would just have to find a way to solve that problem.

When she came that Sunday, as quickly as possible we told her of our meeting. She responded very cool about it. Her only response was, "And what did you tell him?"
"We told him that we would have to first consult with you," I answered. She immediately switched the topic and told us she had gotten a couple of other church groups to come in but was waiting on the authorities to get them the security clearance needed.

The following week Tuesday, true to his word the Chaplain was there and sent for us. He used a different strategy this time. He asked us to come in one at a time. When each person went in and answered his questions, he would send him out through another office. He didn't want to risk any collaboration with each other. I was last. When I went into him, he pretended as if all the other guys had agreed to go with him. What he figured was that the other guys would go whichever way I went so he had me in last, but that backfired on him. I said no. I could see that he was visibly shaken. He went on to explain the benefit of going with him and again I tuned him down. It was when he was getting up that I realized he had ended the meeting and I was then taken back to the cell block. By this, all the other guys were wondering what was happening because it seemed as if I had spent an extra-long time with him.

All of them gathered around me in my cell with great anticipation in their eyes. The question was simple, "What did you say to him?"
"I told him no" was my response. Then they all breathed a sigh of relief. They all went on to tell of their experience with him and the veiled

threats and promises he made. For a moment in the office with him, I was kind of tending to believe him about the guys being willing to go along with him. But being with them I was convinced that that was not so, because he also tried that tactic with me too. This encounter did not do much good for my faith in Christians. He was a leader in one of the biggest denominations and he was lying to, and manipulating us like that. I was very hurt and disappointed. "God, is this what Christianity is all about? How can I be a part of something like this?"

The only response I received from the Lord was, "Focus on Me".

We could not wait for Sunday to give Sister Allison the drama. I walked her up to the caravan with the officer and gave her a short version of what happened, and I could hear her shouting a big "Thank You, Lord" in her heart. That was very comforting to know that someone else was talking to God just like me, and I could hear them too. Church took on a new dimension that morning. The presence of the Lord was so rich. And all that week I just basked in it. It was not until about a couple of years later that we saw the Chaplain again, and he did not come to see us. We just saw him slipping in and slipping out. By this time, we were having our daily prayer meeting out in the yard. No congregating was allowed but we got the go-ahead from the Superintendent because of how impressed he was by us trying to have our service and not waiting on outsiders. There was a lot more for the authorities to be thankful for: the fights, escape attempts, and wounding among inmates that used to be a part of our daily lives were now almost non-existent. Inmates were voluntarily participating in our prayer meetings and Sunday services, even though they had different motives. The Lord told me that it was okay for them to use us like that. The truth is they were hearing the Word anyway. And that was the most important. With this, the authorities began to loosen up the restrictions because the inmates were a lot more cooperative; they were going to church and prayer meetings. So even in the odd times, we were allowed out of the cells for such activities. And "Elder Thirteen" would keep them in check. This was my new title as everything about the brethren automatically passed through me; it just happened that way.

- - -

A lot started happening at the institution. I began to learn how to read and write. Very soon after the murder attempt, I was in one of my regular conversations with the Lord. He said to me, "Now that you won't be doing what you used to do, what are you going to do?" This was the first time that the reality of me being illiterate hit home. My God, can you believe that? Twenty-three years old and functionally illiterate. Unbelievable! I couldn't go back to the hustle or that way of life. I had to change. But do what? I am basically unable to read and write, so where do I start?

Sometimes, even when I was not directly talking to the Lord, He listened to my thoughts. He said to me, "Learn to read and write." "How do I do that?", I responded.
"See that inmate reading that newspaper? Go stand beside him and listen to him", He instructed. I obeyed and listened. When he was finished, the Lord asked me to take the paper and read it. Obediently, I borrowed the paper and asked the inmate to show me where he was reading. He did and I suddenly realized that I could remember everything that he read and was able to match what I heard him say with the print on the paper. Wow!!! This was neat. So, I kept practicing that every day. At night the other inmates in the cell would read and I would do the same thing with the Bible.

During this period of time an inmate was transferred to Gun Court, from another prison, for security reasons. I did not know him personally, but he was from my area. And we got to talk about him teaching me how to read and write, and he agreed. He started the class with one student— me; later, another inmate joined. But he was only willing to teach me. So, everything he taught me I taught the other inmates. After a few weeks, he got frustrated and stopped the class with me. It was then that we realized that we were under observation. Several inmates came to me and wanted to know why we stopped the class. I told them, "No teacher." So, I went to have a conversation with the "teacher" who later agreed to continue the classes, and to our surprise we had about twelve students.

However, there was a problem. Not all the students were at the same level academically, and a lot of them started to drop out. After much discussion, we decided that we had something good going on here. With the encouragement of a couple of progressive officers, we decided to contact JAMAL (*Jamaica Movement for the Advancement of Literacy*) and ask for their help. The superintendent at the time was very willing to assist because he saw the benefit of having some sort of program in the institution. It was not going to cost them anything and a couple of officers were volunteering to specially monitor us. Within a few weeks, with the red tape cleared, my friend from JAMAL came with a team to evaluate what we had and were doing. They were excited about what they saw and immediately started to put plans in place to make it an official JAMAL program. Teacher trainers were brought in, and entry tests and evaluations were done to determine who could qualify as a teacher and who would be going into which class. The thing is, we had about 35 candidates for the four classes, but no-where to keep them. We settled for two classes in the church caravan and the other two in the corridor over on the other side of the Remand section. Naturally, I was in grade one, which was where most of us were placed. I didn't care. I was learning, and that was all that mattered.

Also, there was a new problem that no one anticipated. The school had to have a principal. The principal needed to be someone who would be able to keep these guys in check to make sure that the visiting teachers were respected, and to prevent trafficking of contraband between teachers and inmates. I was at the forefront of organizing everything and was the one who was acquainted with everything. The lot fell on me, and no one objected. In the middle of all this, my desire to learn was being severely hampered. There was always something to call me away from my class to go help with. The good thing though was that the teachers and I developed a very good relationship, and they seemed to be calling for my assistance for just about everything.

I was handling things quite well, if I may say so. We had a fully certified JAMAL School. From time to time, we would receive visits from the higher-ups, both from JAMAL and the Ministry of National Security, just to see how things were going. Not in their wildest dream did they imagine that anything like this could have happened– no, not in Gun Court. Just over a year ago, this place was the most dreaded institution in the Jamaica penal system, with a very successful school and a church that was very much alive. Both inmates and warders were coming to us for prayers. Some even came for "read ups." Believe it or not, a lot of false doctrines were creeping in. I was not aware of the specifics, but God would give me a bad feeling about things, and I would stand my ground. Quite a few of the inmates were backsliders and had their version of what should be happening in the church.

Within a year I had moved up through all four classes. I scored high on all the tests and was the teachers' star student. We even had a graduation. I can vaguely remember anything about that besides the fact that they allowed our families to come and watch us like guinea pigs in a pen. However, it made the inmates proud of themselves. They never had anything like this before. Most of us were from the inner-city and never completed school, so having a graduation and getting a certificate was a very big deal. I can't remember if my family was there. Regardless, I had other things on my mind. I was very comfortable with having God and was hungry– very hungry– for more learning. I was planning way ahead of this and had already approached the teachers for books to do some subjects in the JSC (*Jamaica School Certificate*) exams. God and I were having lots of fun in this. He gave me a solid kick-start and now I was unstoppable. Education was fun and I wanted more– everything I could get! God is a Father, and being that I was sure at times He was annoyed at me, the way I just kept pushing.

Now that I no longer needed to be in class, I had a lot of spare time. I didn't want that; I wanted to study! There was one major hitch though: I did not have a teacher. By this time, I had gotten books for five JSC subjects: Mathematics, English, History, Biology, and Civics. In discussing my problem with one of the teacher trainers, she suggested that I could still come to the JAMAL classes, and she would give me some special attention. This was good, *very good.* And this was when I embarked on my JSC studies. For things she could not help me with, she would refer me to another teacher. And before long they were all coaching me. When it was time for exams the Ministry of Education allowed me to take the exams in the prison. And much to the delight of everyone, and especially the teachers who helped me, I was successful in all five exams: Maths (Distinction); History (Distinction); Biology (Credit); Civics (Credit); English (Pass).

By this, the authorities were seeing the benefit of the program and employed someone to oversee it, from a Ministry level and wanted to duplicate it in the other prisons. They tried but it was not so successful. The individuals involved weren't as excited and committed as we were at Gun Court. We put our lives into it and the teacher trainers were very encouraged by our enthusiasm and zeal. But I believed that the real reason was because it was God who gave birth to this thing and was overseeing it. While leading this program, there was nothing that I would do without expressly discussing it with God. And sure enough, He would guide me every step of the way. On several occasions, it was discovered that I was being set up and the enemy's plans would fail.

After my success at the JSC exams, I was even hungrier and wanted more. This was when they all said that I was crazy. Because I was so successful with the JSC I wanted to do some O'Levels, London exams. Yes, you read right– I wanted to do some O'Levels now.

The friend that had helped me to start the school wrote poems and I was encouraged to try it. It sure worked. He came up with this brilliant idea that we could enter some of our poems in the Festival Poetry Competition. That first year I did not make the grade, but he won a bronze award. However, the next year was going to be a whole lot different. We co-wrote a play called "*Jamaican Struggle*." The adjudicator was so impressed with it that they decided to come by the Gun Court. Again, the red tape issue came up. This time it was not so bad because they were given unlimited access and began to do a lot of workshops with us. They brought in all the big names in the drama business. I found out afterwards that most of them who came did so out of curiosity. Gun Court? Guys doing drama in Gun Court? But their visits paid off. They imparted a lot of knowledge and skill onto us, and we learned so much that we won the prestigious National Award.

As a result of this win, we were expected to perform at the Ward Theatre. It was the tradition of the JCDC (*Jamaica Cultural Development Commission*) that the winning drama piece is viewed at the Ward Theatre. This was where the issue came up: *Tradition* vs *Security*. However, one of the great trade-offs with the visits from all the Drama World Big-Wigs was that they seemed to know all the right buttons to push to make things happen. And they did. The authorities finally capitulated and allowed us to perform at the Ward Theatre. The cast was very small; only three of us and all we had as props were two cardboard maps of Jamaica and Africa, and a coconut oil zinc pan for our drum. There was a lot of speculation about escaping. Two of us were convicted of gun crimes and were doing two or more life sentences– I could understand the fear. The public would freak out if one of us had even tried to escape. I was confident though that all would be well. Of course, *Big Daddy* had assured me that all would be well. And I told the authorities that it would be so, and they believed me. No one in the audience knew that we were inmates from the real Gun Court. They thought that the name, "Gun Court Cultural Movement" was some community group who just wanted to make a statement with the name. After the performance we all headed home (Gun Court) and all was well, as Big Daddy assured us.

We had an award-winning cultural group and all of Jamaica knew it. It did not change our conditions anyway. A school of proven success, a national award-winning drama group, and a Church that was winning souls and showing the power of God, and we were still doing life sentences without parole, and sleeping in a 5x8 cell with two other inmates. This kind of put me in a mood and I started to look back on some of our progress and incidents. That's when it dawned on me that God had actually allowed me to be speedily sentenced. The way the tension at GP about me chasing the warder built up to a climax was unsettling. The warder that was always there to save me was off duty. I was easy-pickings. Therefore, if I was taken back to GP that evening after the court hearing I would have been dead meat. I absolutely would not have survived. These officers were hungry for blood and it would have been mine. And the reality of my life being saved because of that was just hitting home. The prospect of going back to the GP was very chilling. And here I was brooding about being still locked up in the cell. Being at Gun Court was a hundred times better than facing those blood thirsty officers at GP. I needed to be more thankful.— yet another time Big Daddy showed Himself strong for me.

- - -

I remember one day while we were having one of our outdoor prayer meetings, one of the brethren came to me and said that the Lord told him in a dream last night that he had received the gift of healing.

"Ok, sounds good", I responded coolly. Just about then an inmate was coming in from the doctor. He had a condition on his hand, and everyone was saying that it was leprosy. I didn't know what it was, but it was spreading down from his wrist and passing his elbow. All the ointments, creams, and other medications he received were of no use. As a matter of fact, we felt that they were making it worse. He walked right into the midst of the meeting and stood beside us. I turned and looked at him and turned to the *healer* and said, "You said that God gave you the gift of healing?"
"Yes!" he said with much confidence.
The next thing I said to him shook him up. I said, "This man needs healing, so heal him." About ten or fifteen of us were standing there, and he seemed unsure of what to do. So, I repeated it, "Heal him." Looking back now, I think that was a bit cruel to put him on the spot like that. But as God would have it, I did right.

He suddenly grabbed the guy with both his hands and said, "Heal up, heal up, heal up!" three times and let him go. One of the things I learned early in my walk with the Lord is that you do what you are told and let God do the rest. None of us could heal anyone, so all we had to do was pray. And that he did. He looked at me and I gave my approval. They all were satisfied.

About ten minutes later, the prayer meeting came to an end. Exercise time was over and each of us went to our respective block. This inmate with the hand condition had to wrap his hand in a towel two or three times a day to contain the petrification leaking from his hand. However, he realized that his hand had stopped leaking by the time we were back for the last hour of the day. He called my attention to it. After inspecting it I kept my cool. But the next morning there was shouting and noise on his block. When there was any such kind of uproar, we all assumed that it was a kind of fight or something like that. And the warders rushed to the scene with batons, ready to start breaking some heads. Since the establishment of the Church and schools, there had never been a fight. So, naturally this drew a lot of attention.

When they got there all the inmates were surrounding the inmate that had the hand condition, only this time there was no towel on his hand, and you could not distinguish which hand was sick. Everyone was curious. He kept shouting, "Di Christian dem pray fi mi, di Christian dem pray fi mi (*The Christians prayed for me– the Christians prayed for me*)!" No one could deny it. The evidence was there staring them in the face. Both his hands were the same now; there was not even a scar on the hand that was sick,

It was frightening. I had never seen anything like this. I have heard of people getting healed in church but to see it right here, in the Gun Court, before our very eyes was crazy. How else could I explain it? This was not a little headache we're talking about. This was big. Man, this was *BIG*. I was numbed. I didn't know what to say to the Lord. For days I just sat in wonderment and awe, not saying a word to the Lord. But what could I say? Sitting and having a conversation with God was one thing, but to witness a miracle like this was a whole different kettle of fish. Both inmates and warders alike were hounding us wanting us to lay hands on them. Everyone was looking at us very strange. They would only approach if they needed prayer.

One day, as I was sitting in my cell just to avoid the curious stares, an inmate came to me and said that he needed deliverance. Now, I didn't have a clue as to what that was. When I asked him what the problem was, he said that a bee had gone up in his head through his ear. "Why don't you let them take you to the doctor?" I asked him.
"No," he said. "Is not a real bee. It is a demon. And him a blow - up mi head. Im wing dem a buzz in deh (*It is not a real bee. It's a demon.*

He's blowing up my head. His wings are buzzing around in there)!" I just sat there and listened to him. He then started to make this strange humming sound and shouted, "Imma come now, tek im out (*He is coming out now. Take him out*)!" All I could remember was this guy, a living human being, changing into a frog-like creature right there in front of me, sitting on my bunk, large face, bumpy skin and all. If you thought the miracle was scary, this was indescribable! I remembered nothing about prayer. After some time, I don't remember how long, God delivered him. I don't remember the details. But I saw him delivered and was laying on the ground, and his skin and face gradually returned to normal. This guy was a hit man and didn't want his experience to be known. But he committed his life to the Lord, received the baptism of the Holy Spirit and was speaking in tongues right there.

God was doing something that we could not understand, but we just rolled along with Him. One day during the prayer meeting, one of the Christian brethren was leaving the meeting to go to court. He asked us to pray for him, so I asked him, "What do you want God to do?" He said that he wanted to go home because he was there for a few years and was not guilty. I said to him, "Listen to me carefully. The judge is going to ask you this same question. What do you want him to do? You must give him the same answer; nothing more, nothing less."
"That's it?" he inquired.
I said, "Yes. God has already gone ahead of you to court." That afternoon he came back for his things and was screaming on the top of him voice that the same thing that I said would happen, happened and he was free.

Prophesying and speaking into people's lives were becoming a natural thing. We were able to summon the families of inmates who had abandoned them to come and visit them. With this Sister Allison had gotten about five more groups consisting of all kinds of denominations. But God had to remove most of them. They were causing more confusion than anything else. Like me, most of the guys had no church experience and were very gullible. The other groups were coming with their denominations' doctrines and most of us were just learning to read the Bible by ourselves and Sister Allison was not able to do anything else but preach. It was against the prison's policy for her to be with a specific group of us. Only the teachers were allowed, and that was during the week. So, it was up to me to allow Big Daddy to teach me the Word.

Three of us started to have our own Bible study. One of the guys was the son of a pastor and that helped a bit. But I sooner had to scrap it because they were listening to some false teachings trying to impose it on us. So, what we started to do was to have our scriptures ready for Sister Allison and she would, the next time she visited, do a teaching on the topic. That was the best and we looked forward to it each time. The group from the Holiness Church was really good. They were preaching the same gospel Sister Allison was preaching. The basics of their message were holiness and living right.

The Roman Catholics were a bit different. They didn't have a Gospel as such. They were much more interested in our welfare and would bring us clothes and other personal stuff like soap, toothpaste, shampoo, etc. These items were very critical because most of us were not being visited by either friends or family. We would be in there for the rest of our lives, so they abandoned us. We're supposed to receive these items from the authorities. But, according to them, they were not able to provide it because the budget was not adequate. So, thank God for the Church Groups, and the authorities capitalized on it. These people were like literal angels. They made us feel so loved. Some of them would go to our homes and counsel our families, even though some of us lived in some very dangerous places. They did it anyway. One young man even went as far as paying for a Correspondence Bible Course for me out of his pocket and we became such good friends that he ended up being my best friend. He saw my hunger for learning and fed it. We kept close in touch. He ended up being something of a mentor to me.

- - -

After I had finished with JSC I wanted to do The O'Levels. The problem with this was the lack of books and teachers. Again, the teacher trainers and the visiting churches stepped in and were able to provide with the books for Traditional Maths, West Indian History, and English Language. The plan was that the teachers would get me the pass papers to work on. I would then give the work back to them and they would get some High School teacher friends to mark them for me.

I cannot, forget my mom paid for the exams for me in January because she used the money that was for house rent and food for the rest of the family. However, she was not able to come visit me. The prison caused her much stress, so I told her that it was okay for her not to come because God was working things out for my good. I understood. The one time she came she almost had a nervous breakdown. And I definitely would not have that happening to her. I wanted to do the exams in June, but everyone advised me that I could not do it in less than six months. High school students took four to six years, even with teachers, and this was not like JSC. The work was ten times harder. They all advised me to do History and/or English. Mathematics? No way! Traditional Math had three parts: Arithmetic and Trigonometry, Geometry, and Algebra. They were all three-hour papers, and to even pass the subject one would have to pass all three sections. At this point I had to learn how to tune out the naysayers because I was sure I was going to do them.

So, after the payments were made in January, I buckled down into the pass papers provided by the JAMAL Teacher trainers. Another issue surfaced. I needed a lot of paper for the rough work. I started to use papers from the JAMAL program, but they were also not enough. So, each time I went for occasional exercise, I would pick up whatever pieces of paper I saw on the ground, brushed off the dirt that was on it, folded and put it in my pocket. When they all saw me doing that it became a common knowledge that I was losing my mind. A lot of people began to laugh at me and say that I was picking up what I could not manage. Big Daddy and I had a good laugh out of it, though. I was going full-steam ahead. I needed to pass these exams, with good grades too. The Lord had already assured me that if I trusted Him, we would go through it together and be successful. One other thing that the Lord showed me was that I should never study and go straight for the exams. I should give myself some time to relax between studying and sitting for the exam. This I did. I stopped studying exactly four weeks before the exams started. And all I would do was rest, read other books, including the Bible, have conversations with Big Daddy, and sleep. When exam time came up, everyone was rooting for me, even people who did not like me— and that felt *good*.

The first exam was English Language. At first, I was a little nervous, but my confidence grew as I went into it. It was a two-and-a-half-hour paper, and I was out of there in less than two hours. The exam center was set up at GP. It had better accommodations and space, and a few inmates there were also taking the exams. When I was taken back to Gun Court everyone was waiting to hear how I did. No one knew that anything like this could happen in Gun Court. God was opening doors we could have never imagined. The remaining exams were a breeze. I completed each one in less than two hours, including the three-hour ones. God was opening my mind and confidence to so many things I never had a clue about. I was now writing poems and plays; leading a drama group; managing a school; and pastoring a Church. Just a few years ago, as the Jamaican saying goes, "*I never know 'A' from bull foot.*" And God was not finished yet. As a matter of fact, He was just getting started.

The exam results were out and to everyone's surprise, I got an "A" in Math, the very subject they all said I should not do, especially the person appointed to coordinate the so-called "Educational Program." In fact, I also got an "A" in History, and a "C" in English Language. There was a great jubilation for me in the prison by the inmates, but the officers were jealous of me. Before long, they started to accuse me of acting as if I was better than them. So, I kept to myself and close to my cell. When the news reached Sister Allison and the other Church groups and the teachers, they started to treat me with a new level of respect.

The Government began to set up a system to review our cases and a team was coming in to interview inmates to determine if there was any merit in a review. And yes, there were quite a few. There were people that were there just for being in the wrong place at the wrong time. And they deserve the review to be released. I was guilty, so I was not complaining. I would love to be released, yes, but I had accepted my fate. Sometimes, whenever I complained, the Lord would say that I shouldn't complain about anything because if I don't walk out the gates, I would be going up with Him, and I was satisfied with that.

The hope and expectations in the prison were taking on a new dimension. A few cases were being reviewed and the anticipation of the possibility of being released was feverish. But there were those among us who already knew that we would not be included in the process. Our reputations had already preceded us but the fact that some of us were going home was enough to cause high hopes.

Now with the O'Levels behind me, I began to wonder "What next?" I was doing the Correspondence Course my friend had paid for and it was almost completed. It had seven levels and I was on the last one, so I started to investigate the possibility of moving up to the A 'Levels. This, however, proved a lot more difficult than expected. It was a lot more difficult to get books. But, with the Lord, there had to be something else that I could do. I don't remember how or where the information came to me, but I learned that the Engineering Department at the then *College of Art Science and Technology* (C.A.S.T.)– now the *University of Technology*– offered a part time course that I would be qualified for, if I could get to go. I don't know what had gotten into me, but I started nagging the Lord about going, so He said that I should apply. Do you understand how ridiculous and crazy this was? Here I was doing two life sentences, still considered a major security risk, and I was talking about going to College outside. But God is a specialist at working with impossible situations. I got an application and sent it in with a letter about who I really was. And then I got the response of a lifetime. The essence was that if I was allowed to come, I would be accepted. This was where the real problem was, getting permission to go. Absolutely, no one thought that it was a good idea. Only Sister Allison said that she would be praying.

When I asked the Superintendent's permission he just simply laughed and said that if I think that the Ministry of National Security and the Ministry of Education would allow something like this, and I confidently said "Yes."

He said, "OK. I'll put in the paperwork for you." He paused, and then said, "What on earth am I doing?" He turned to me and said, "This is my job. You want me to join you in the cell?" With the excitement building up in me, I responded, "Boss, the Lord told me to ask you." He mumbled something and dismissed me. Now came the waiting and praying period. The response from the Education Ministry came first, passing it off to the Ministry of National Security. And the Ministry of Nation Security passed it on to the Department of Correctional Services, that had direct responsibilities for prisons. The Correctional Department then passed it off to the Superintendent saying that I was his prisoner and was best able to determine how to handle it.

He called me to his office and told me the whole story. He said that if he was going to take the risk, I would have to convince him that he was doing the right thing. I proceeded to remind him how we made him proud, when, under my leadership, three of us went to Ward Theater and nothing happened, and how he and a handful of officers walked with eighteen of us, all doing life sentence, on the road from Gun Court to the Little Theater at night, to perform. That had never been done in the history of the Penal System in Jamaica. I could see that that got to him. Then, I showed him all the awards and trophies we had won in the Festival Competitions that had adorned his office. And that did it. One thing though he would have to get a recommendation from the Chaplain, the same Chaplain who we had not seen for years, and who was mad at me for preventing the brethren from being confirmed by him to be a part of his Church. That didn't sound too good. Regardless, I was glad and grateful so far for the fact that the way was being cleared for me, and I was on cloud ninety-nine.

This great feeling was gradually fading when we realized the Chaplain could not be found. I later found out that all that was left to be done was for him to sign the document. The months dragged on and in one conversation with the Superintendent, I learned that the Chaplain went on extended vacation. On hearing this, one begs to wonder, was this deliberate to get back at me? After all, he knew about the need for him to sign the document before he left. His office was just down the road. He did not come back for a full year. Maybe he thought that the authorities and the College would give up on me and cancel my application. So, I sent a letter to the College apologizing that I was not able to take up the offer and if they would be still open for me. The resounding response was "Yes." So, upon the Chaplain's return, he was promptly presented with the document for his signature. Even though he hesitated, he could not refuse. And *BLESS GOD*!!! I was registered to attend C.A.S.T.!

I was not even thinking about fees and costs. I was not aware that

God had already gone ahead of me and had prepared everything. I had become good friends with a couple of the members of the review team, *Dawn Walker* and *Blossom Dixon*. When it was drawing near, I was told by one of them that a very big corporate law firm, *Myers, Fletcher and Gordon*— one of the biggest in the Caribbean— through *Mrs. Dorothy Pine-McClarty* had heard about me and my efforts and had decided to sponsor ALL my fees and cost to attend college. If I was allowed to go to school my finances would be totally covered. They didn't even know me, had never seen me before but was just obedient to what God had laid in their hearts. Their only request was that I do well and provide them with an annual report for their files. I didn't even know who they were. This was mind-boggling. I knew that God was using people on my behalf, but these people who were so on top of their game would allow themselves to be used by God like this was without measure. [*Oh my God, You never cease to be so amazing.*]

During the time I was waiting to go to school the excitement and tension was unbearable. Everyone was talking: some about the miracle, and some about whether I was going to run away. They were the ones waiting for that to happen to wreck the rest of the programs. As far as they were concerned there should be no programs here. This place was not for rehabilitation. Prisoners were to be treated like dogs. Yet, the official name of the Institution was *Gun Court Rehabilitation Center.* There were no rehabilitation programs here except the school, Church, and drama group, all created, designed, developed, implemented, and run by inmates. A few officers skillfully found their niche and came along for the ride. That was good because they played a very vital role in getting the authorities to accept them. [*Anyway, Big Daddy, you and I know that it happened because of you.*]

D-Day was drawing close and some of the visiting Church Brethren assisted me with some proper clothes to wear. Those I had for a few years did not look so proper and were very noticeable. Thank God for generous people. At the same time, there was a lot of discussion among the staff as to how this would go. The regulation requires that when an inmate is being taken outside the compound, he should be escorted by at least two officers, and at least one must be armed. For the warders this opportunity was going to provide a lot of overtime. Then, there is the speculation about whether the guard chosen to escort me would be sitting in the classroom with me or not. Then there was the matter of the handcuffs. Would/should it be used? I tried not to pay any attention to these speculations. All I cared about was that I was going to college.

D-Day was here, and I was supposed to go to the orientation class at 2pm. Up until then there was nothing being said about escort duty. I tried not to trouble myself with that— It was not my problem. "But please Lord, don't let them use that against me."

So, at 1pm I got ready and went to the Superintendent's office. He seemed a little surprised when I said that I was ready to go to school. He leaned back in his chair, put his hand in his pocket, took out some money and handed it to me, and said, "Gwaan to school (*Go to school*)." What?! Was I hearing right? Was this really happening? This is very much illegal inside the prison for inmates to have money in their possession; and to have the Superintendent himself putting money in your hand was way outside anything one could imagine. And now he was saying that I should be going. This was really what blew my mind. I said to him, "But, boss you know that I can't just walk through the gates like that." He acknowledged and took up the phone and called the front gate and said, "Inmate Vivian Talbot will be coming down. Let him out!" I don't know what the response on the phone was, but he was not very pleased and barked, "Who is the Superintendent here?" He slammed down the phone, and turned to me and said, "What you waiting for? Gwaan to school!".

I beat a hasty retreat out of his office. But then I started thinking, 'What if this is a setup?' The route from his office to the gate is a super restricted area and no inmate, at any time at all should be seen in it. But then, in reasoning with myself, I was thinking that he was a good man and I didn't believe that he would sink that low, after everything. So, with much trepidation and excitement, as I approached the gate, what greeted me at the gate was a very beautiful sight. Talking about God giving you honor over your enemies; the guards at the gates to open it for me were my archenemies. They never let a moment pass without antagonizing me. On several occasions, they would threaten that they were going to make sure that I died in prison. They were the ones who would be opening the gates to let me go to school. As I approached them, I could feel the hatred like a physical force emanating from them. I calmly walked to them and paid my respects while watching them open the gate. As I stepped across the threshold, I could hear them say-ing, "Mmm, him gone now. Im not coming back (*Mmm. He's gone now. He is not coming back*)."

It immediately started to rain and I held up my face to the rain and said, "Lord, You hear that? We are going to let them eat their words." Even if I was planning to run, and I did think about it a few times, after hearing them making that statement I would never give them the pleasure of being right. Never!

I walked the quarter mile to *Cross Roads* in a trance. At this time, the rain had stopped. It was God's way of showing that He was there with me and blessing me. The entire evening was an unreal experience. I went to the orientation desk and collected my package. I was to have classes for two days. One day was for two hours and the other was ten hours. I was enrolled in the Part-time Electrical Engineering (Power) Program. This was a four-year certificate course for working students. After the orientation was over at about 8pm, I just walked around a bit, just to get a *lay of the land*, where my classes were going to be, the cafeteria, the chapel, the main office, the student union office, and the library. These were the places that I would need to go to on occasion. I decided to leave at about 9pm. The trip back was quick. It took about twenty minutes. On my way back I was like a homing pigeon. There was haste in my steps, and I was wondering if I had pushed it too much by staying until 9pm.

When I reached the gates there was no one there. So, I knocked and shouted, "Let me in!" That sounded so strange— A prisoner coming to the prison gates and begging to be allowed back in. The "wrecking crew" was still on duty, and they let me in, only this time they grabbed me under my arms, one on each side with my feet barely touching the ground and ran with me and unceremoniously threw me into the cell. So I said, "Hey, What with the attitude?"

"We're just making sure," they responded simply then slammed the cell door, and off they went. There was a tangible quietness. One could literally feel the expectations and questions that everyone wanted to ask but no one did. And that was fine with me. I was in mental turmoil and needed to settle myself. Here, I was back in my cell. Being thrown in the cell after I voluntarily walked back here. I could have gone anywhere, but I chose to come back. And this is the way they treated me and I wept. Why? Because of the disrespect? I don't think so... As a matter of fact, thinking back, I am not even sure. But one thing was for sure, I was one big bundle of emotional and mental confusion. It was then that I started to evaluate what I was getting into.

This was my first day and I was having some serious trouble making the readjustments back to prison life. To make this thing work I would have to learn to make this transition twice daily. The lifestyle and per-sonality I lived while in prison would not ever work on the outside and vice versa. I was beginning to understand why a lot of guys who leave prison find it so hard to adjust to life on the outside. The taste of freedom I just experienced had a bittersweet taste. To be able to walk around and talk to anyone, without a guard watching your every move is a glorious feeling. After five years of being locked up, it felt great and beautiful. Yes, beautiful. On the other hand, however, it was very bitter considering the way I was treated. But I would have to learn to deal with it, and I knew that the Lord would be there with me. With these thoughts in mind, I fell asleep.

The imagery and sights of the outside were indelibly imprinted in my mind. Everything I looked at seemed so drab and ugly compared to the things I saw out there and had in my head. I couldn't wait to start going to class in just two more days. I was unable to eat the breakfast they gave us. I had no appetite. Right after breakfast I was deluged with attention and questions. Most of the inmates were just plain curious: how did I feel; did I go get some sex; did they know that I was a prisoner; am I going to run? And the questions went on. It was a bit surprising to hear some of the other inmates standing up for me, shutting down some of the questions on my behalf. But most of all the consensus was that I should play it cool because what I do with this opportunity was going to set the stage for them whether they would be able to get a break too. One thing for sure, there was a new surge of hope and desire to participate in any program or positive activities in the prison. There were no problems from the inmates anymore. Everyone was cool and complied with every order and instruction from the warders.

I must go report to the Boss himself. I went to his office and one look at his face said it all. For the first time in my life, there was someone who was proud of me for who I was and what I had done. And that felt good. We talked for about an hour. It was more encouraging and challenged me to stand with him and make him proud. All the naysayers were now silenced. They were all afraid to touch my case because of my reputation. At one time they were saying that people like me could not be rehabilitated and that the church and school activities were just a sham. The Superintendent was assigned to Gun Court because he was a strict and firm senior officer and that he was the best man for the job. They all were surprised that he was so willing to go along with the programs we were building. And worst of all, allowing me to go to school caught them off-guard. Later I heard that they were now earmarking him for the top job in the department, which he did get, by the way. No one in the history of the penal system was ever able to achieve what he did, in terms of rehabilitation, especially with abso-lutely no help or resources from the "Powers that be." Remember it all started with the idea that "it is red; because it is dread." Now inmates were attending college all on their own, while still doing life sentences.

The whole idea of books came up and that's when I told him about the scholarship from the law firm. He was a little annoyed that I did not pass it through him, but cooled down once I told him that I had nothing to do with it and all money would go straight to the school and not in my hands. I can understand his annoyance because it would not be taken kindly by the higher-ups to know that an inmate would be handling so much money in the prison. The whole issue of bribery was a touchy subject.

After the talk with the Superintendent, I went to meet with Dawn and Blossom from the review board and talked to her about the booklist, which she took and said that she would handle it. Classes would be starting in a couple of days, and she assured me that I would be getting my books in time. The first day at school was one of the evening classes. While in the class, it took some time to get used to everyone around me, but then I realized that no one was paying any attention to me, because as far as they were concerned, I was just another working guy who wanted to upgrade himself. And that made it so much easier. The day ended with me dreading the previous experience of being thrown into the cell. On my arrival I was treated with a lot more respect and was allowed to get some "*fresh up*" before I was locked down.

I then started settling into my rhythm, and it became a normal routine to see me come and go in the days. And life started to take on a new meaning. I was now experiencing what it was to really go to school and being taught by a real teacher, had class assignments and did real exams in a real classroom. I buckled down and tried to fall in the grove of things. I realized that I was going to need Big Daddy now more than ever. I had to stay back to do most of my assignments because I had to use the library a lot to complete my assignments. There was nowhere in prison to do research. But I had to take it easy. I couldn't push it on to them so fast; got to work it in and take it slow. But I started to pick up the pace as I got the hang of things. One day I was talking to the Lord about the fact that this was not Gun Court and that I was not in class among the other inmates who were not better than I was, but I was now among people who had their degrees and were just doing some upgrades. I had to excel, I had to be successful, not for my sake but for the other guys inside who were putting their hope in me. So, in our conversation, I was just talking to the Lord about it and that I couldn't afford to fail anything.

He said to me, "As long as you stay committed to me you will never fail."
"Wow, that's it?" I responded.
"It's not as easy as it sounds. It's going to take a lot of hard work, and sacrifice," He replied.
"I can do that," I replied. So, the conversation went on. I became aware of what I was in for. So, I buckled down. No more excitement and exhilaration because I was on the road. There was a road ahead and a goal to achieve. So, the routine continued and my first year flew by before you could say, "Who said it."

- - -

The end-of-year exams were a lot easier than I had expected, and when the results came out, I got straight A's. This was a great excitement for me because I was continuing on the winning streak. My memory was clicking like a computer. Once I saw it, I'd remember it. And to take it up a few notches, due to my results I was offered a scholarship to move up from part-time to full-time. I was being offered the opportunity to do the three-year Full-time Diploma course. The Superintendent was the first to know and he was more excited than I was and immediately gave his blessings. Mrs. McClarty was also very excited and promised that they would match anything that was going to be needed. So, came the new school year. I was going to be a fulltime student at C.A.S.T.

When I started classes, it dawned on me that the year of being in the part time program was just practice for the fulltime program. Going to class for ten hours a week was nothing like going to class every day for the week for forty-two hours. We were having seven subjects each week. This was when the Lord taught me how to work with a timetable. I built that timetable and stuck to it to the letter. Then, the Lord told me that was the main reason most students were not very successful. They were not organized and lacked discipline. So, I stuck to it. And it paid off. At the close of the first year, when the results came out, I was on top again: four *A*'s and three *B*s. That year I won the award for Academic Excellence, and the Derrick Dunn Trophy. These came with a cash award, which went into my scholarship fund.

Every end of year, the UCCF (*University and Colleges Christian Fellowship*), a group of Christian students on campus, would go to the Blue Mountains Peak for a retreat. They would have a glorious time and I used to hear the testimonies of their experiences at the midday meetings. I became so jealous. So, during one of my sit-downs with the Lord, I brought up the subject of me going the next time they were going. To my surprise, He said, "Yes." So, I was wracking my brain on how this would happen. He did not say anything about applying to the authorities for them to allow me. So, I left that part alone.

As the time drew nigh the Lord said nothing further to me. So, I kept asking Him and all He said to me was, "Have I ever let you down before?" "No," I said.

"Then trust me," He said. So, I left it... but not for long.

And again, the conversation was the same, "Have I ever let you down before?"

"No Sir."

"Then trust Me."

In the evening when they were leaving Papine for the Peak I was sitting in my cell brooding. As the time passed, I couldn't hold back. I asked the Lord one more time, and the conversation was the same. But this time, while we were talking, I suddenly found myself at the peak among the other students. This was awesome. I was there with everyone, walking among them, and the Lord said to me, "Make special note of everything that you see and what is happening because they will not believe you when you go to the lunch hour meeting on Monday." How it all went was exciting and the next thing I knew was that I woke up the next morning in my cell. I had no idea how long the trip lasted but it had a lasting effect on me.

When I went to the mid-day meeting, the Lord obviously knew what He was saying because with my big mouth I cut into the conversation among the students that had gone on the trip. I started to speak, not realizing that everyone was giving me this strange look, because they knew that I was not supposed to have been there. There was quietness all over the place and then reality hit home, and I just clammed up. A few people were brave enough to ask how I knew all of that. So, I just simply said that the Lord took me there. It was like a pandemonium broke out and a lot of people were screaming and were all in dismay. Some even stopped talking to me. They had never heard anything like that before. One brother had to say that what I was saying had to be true, because there was no way that I could have described it with such detail.

Anyway, I continued with my studying and I started to make some friends. People started to come to me for study tips and for me to start a study group. By the second year full-time I had this study thing "down pat." My assignments and research papers were showing great results, and my benefactors were so proud of me. Even though that year was supposed to be the toughest in terms of work volume and difficulty, I breezed through very easily. Sticking to the timetable was the perfect solution.

- - -

After going to school from prison for two years, one day I heard them calling my name. I was not going to school that day. When I inquired, I saw one of the officers, who worked in the office, with a sheet of legal document in his hand. Curiously, I inquired what it was. He said, "Time to go home." I was confused. But it was true. I was released and sent to an hostel to live in for the next few weeks. Two weeks later I received the document from the Governor General for my full and unconditional release. That took me without warning. When I was at the hostel, I started having conversations with Sister Allison about where I was going to be living. I had nowhere else to go but to my mom. What she said however, made a lot of sense. With my new lifestyle and going to school, living at my mom's would be counterproductive. But I had nowhere else to go. I had no family that would be willing to take up that responsibility. And bless her soul, Sister Allison said that she would do it.

I couldn't understand how someone like her could take me into her home, just like that, even when she knew the type of person I was. There was absolutely no way that I would have done it. *No way*. So, after I was fully released, I went to live with her. She had a son there and thank God for him. He treated me just like a real brother. And that was therapeutic for me. I never had someone like that in my life before. I am not sure if I was doing the right things at times, but Sister Allison and her son showed no sign of displeasure towards me. I finally had a real family.

This move had a very negative impact on me. I had to adjust to *street life* once more, and the individuals who knew me, everyone wanted to know how I came out— thank God, I was not living at mom's. But where I was living posed a different kind of problem. I was now on the wrong side of the political divide, which was very active at the time. But I knew that I was under scrutiny from the guys in the community. They were not too friendly with one of my smaller brothers, but the leadership on the side I was living had a lot of respect for me and was deliberately protecting me from the other young *Turks* who were hungry for the blood of a former *Don*. The thing is that their parents and I were buddies, and they spoke highly of me. Some of them even knew me when they were little kids.

One night as I was coming home, as I walked past the *corner* I heard someone said, "Hey Christian bwoy, come yah (*Hey, Christian boy, come here*)." I immediately started to talk to the Lord about how I should respond.
And the Lord said, "Don't answer." So, I obeyed.
The person repeated the command with more ferocity and just then I heard a commanding voice said to him, "Leave the man alone and gweh bwoy (*Leave the man alone and go, boy*)!" I then heard some very heavy blows being delivered and he started to cry out and beg for mercy. I turned around and saw about twelve other guys beating him with rifle butts and kicks. I just made a hasty retreat to home. When I had walked past the corner I saw no one, so I was very surprised when I turned around and saw so many guys beating the other one. They were defending me, but also were upset that he was disobedient

and revealed their hide out. They were so concealed that I passed them without having a clue that they were there. This young man that received the beating spent over two months in the hospital with several broken ribs and other bones.

A few days later, the Don of the area— his uncle and I were buddies— came to me and apologized for what happened. We had a very healthy conversation, mainly about my brother. This was what we call, "a feel out" because they needed to be sure of where I stood. They could not afford to have me living there if I was still going to be involved. I simply told him that I was not into what they were into. I was now a Christian and going to school. No time for foolishness. He was satisfied with that, and they left me alone... for the time being, at least. I quickly got back in the groove of things. Studying was going well, my involvement in UCCF was beautiful, results and grades splendid. It was during one of these times when UCCF was having one of their weekend seminars that I met with my Source of Light— my benefactor.

He came to be our main speaker for the weekend and I never forgot because that weekend changed my life and perspective of God and my relationship with God forever. He spoke on the topic, "*En Christo.*" I honestly don't remember the contents but his presentation was a different matter. He made three one-hour presentations on the two words without looking at any notes at all. His details, references, and quotes were mind-boggling. I was totally mesmerized. I definitely would love to be able to do that.

So, when it was over I asked him, "How did you do that?"
"You have to study and read other books," he responded.
"Do you have those books?" I inquired.
"Yes," he said.
"Can I come by your house and have a look on those books?" I pressed the issue.

And without a second thought he agreed, "Yes."

So we made arrangements for me to come spend a few days at his house. I had never seen someone with so many books and I spent the next five days on the floor of his library devouring and soaking all I could. I left his house with an insatiable hunger for Bible study that is still there to this day. After leaving my first purchase was a copy of "*Strong's Exhaustive Concordance.*"

My second (full-time) year was the year with the most problems— emotional and mental hardships and a lot of schoolwork. And that was the year I did my best. I won the *Student of the Year Trophy,* the *All-round Excellence,* and *Academics Excellence Awards,* among others. Exam results gave me five "A"s and three "B"s and also an *Honors Certificate.*

During my final year I went to live on campus. I lost focus. This was the year Sister Allison died. It was very difficult for me, and it hit me hard. She died on her knees praying. Living on campus took a whole lot more discipline than I had. I was not studying as rigidly as I was. Despite this, I didn't do that bad, but not as close as I could have done. I totally lost focus and it showed in the exam results. For the seven subjects, I had three "A"s, two "B"s and two "C"s. I missed the *Honors Diploma.*

- - -

A lot of people used to say that they were amazed at the extent of my faith. I learned from the best. I remember one day when it was raining, Sister Allison saw a leak in the living room. She stood there looking down at the bucket she had placed on the spot to collect the water. She raised her head to look at the place where the water was coming from. But then I heard her speaking to the Lord, "Well Lord, there it is. You will have to send someone to fix it." About thirty minutes later a gentleman came knocking on the gate.

She went out there to him and he proceeded to say, "Di rain jus dun fall, you no have no leak you need fi fix (*It just rained. Do you have any leaks that you wanted to fix*)?"
"Oh yes." She responded and took him inside to show him the problem. After he did his inspection, he told her how much it would cost, and what type of material it would need to be fixed. "Circle back to me in about two hours and come for the money," she said simply. This totally caught my attention, because I knew that she didn't have that kind of money around. And I also knew that she did not believe in borrowing money. So what now?

After the workman left, I heard her talking. Yes— it was to the Lord. She was saying, "Ok Lord, you already know that I don't have any money, so you will have to send it through someone to me." Now my curiosity was kicked into overdrive. I was not going to leave her out of my sight for a moment. I just HAD to see what was going to happen. From time to time I had been having conversations with the Lord, but to see it being done in such a natural and literal way was mind blowing. As I waited, I heard someone at the gate again. Now, this nearly freaked me out! Sister Allison called him in and without hesitation he began, "Sister Allison, you know that I am not into this '*God business*' when people say that God talks to them. But today, God talked to me and said that you needed to fix the house and I should give you this." He handed her some money and tried to make a hasty retreat.

Sister Allison stopped him and said, "Hold it! Don't you want to collect your blessings?"
Perplexed, he looked at her and said, "What do you mean?"

Sister Allison then simply rested her hand on his shoulder and said, "Lord bless him seven times what he gave me," and sent him off.

Just as he was leaving the workman was coming in. Sister Allison counted the money she had just received, and it was the exact amount that was needed for the job and material. He just turned around and said, "Going to buy the material right now", and then left. He came back later in the evening and repaired the roof and by nightfall everything was done, or so I thought. Seven days later the man who gave her the money came back to Sister Allison. Fear and trepidation were all over his face.

And again, without any hesitation he started, "Sister Allison mi fraid a yu (*Sister Allison, I am afraid of you*)!" And he kept repeating it over and over. He stretched out his hands and said, "Look here. Exactly seven times, *exactly seven times*. Nuh dat yu pray last week? And see it yah! (*Isn't that what you prayed last week? Now here it is!*)" He kept holding his hand out.

Then Sister Allison just simply said, "But that was what I asked the Lord. What did you expect?" This man's life was then totally changed, and mine too. I never doubted the Lord for one minute. But to see things unfolding in front of me in such a matter-of-fact way could mess a man's head up. This led me into some very serious conversations with the Lord. What I did next was simply take it on for myself. From then on the Lord and I were going to flex together. I was talking to the Lord irrespective of where I was, or the company I was in. Our chill out places were everywhere I was. It was as if I was encased in a cocoon with the Lord, and everyone else was outside. As before my conversations with God were very informal and down to earth.

- - -

At our graduation the Lord did a very strange thing. You know, God always lets your enemies see you prosper in front of them. My name was called about five times for me to collect the awards I won. I was the star of the show. After I got off the stage the detective, that had my first case, and who swore that he would kill me, walked right up to me and said, "I had to come and see if it was really you. O my God, I can't believe it. You sure did come out good." His daughter was graduating too, but he was all over me, and it made me very uncomfortable. Not because I was afraid, but I just did not like the police, and especially him.

School was now over, so what next? My first thought was further studies. But no, not yet. I needed to find a way to thank the Lord, so I told my pastor that I wanted to do the next two years in full-time Ministry. And everyone advised me against it, saying that the first two years after school were the most critical and that was when you could get your big break. Well, that was exactly why I was going to be giving it to the Lord. Now, I would have to find somewhere to live because I would have to move off campus. I found somewhere easily, but the money to pay the bills and other expenses, I believed that God was going to provide. He'd been doing that all along and there was no reason for Him to stop now. And true to His Word people started to contribute to supporting me in Ministry. Individual brethren took on different bills for me: rent, light and water, food, and other day-to-day expenses.

Ministry was good. I started getting a lot of requests to speak at churches, crusades, camps, youth groups, as well as with individuals. My Church was a young church which was a part of an international organization, and the leadership was required to do a lot of travel for training— once or twice per year. And I attended them all and watched how God brought money in as if I had a bank or something. I remembered on one occasion, we were all booked to go to a three-day conference in

Dallas, Texas. The morning of our travel day, before we left that evening, I did not have a cent of the twenty-three thousand dollars needed to cover the expenses. During my conversation (what others might call their devotion) with the Lord before I left for the office, He told me to go sit in a particular chair at the office and wait and watch Him rain money in my lap. Obediently, I went to the office and sat in the chair. The secretary asked me why that chair. So, I told her what the Lord said, and I was obeying it. She thought it was so funny. However, I sat down and waited. After about two hours of waiting I got frustrated and went out to see if I could link up with some business friends of mine in the area. Nothing happened. Tired and miserable I went back to the office to resume my vigil. As I entered, the secretary said, "Where have you been? A gentleman came by and said that you had been friends for a long time, and he was trying to find you for quite a few years. He also said that you should not leave because he'll be back soon." I thanked her and rebuked myself and repented for being disobedient.

A few minutes later he walked in, and yes, we were very good friends, and yes, we hadn't seen each other for quite a few years. As he walked up to me sitting in the chair, he threw an envelope into my lap. Then I immediately remembered the Word of the Lord, "Sit in the chair and watch Me rain money into your lap." This was awesome to see God being so literal. My friend and I spent some time just catching up. When he left, I looked in the envelope and there was almost fifteen thousand in it.

Just as I was talking to the Lord about the remainder of what I needed a young lady from the church came in and saw me. She was aware of the trip that evening and asked me if I got all the money I needed and I said no. Then she asked me how much more I needed. Not wanting to divulge my business I just said, "A lot." Obviously, she was not satisfied with that answer.

Not wanting to sound rude I told her the amount and she just said, "Follow me." Obediently, I followed her. She went straight to the bank, withdrew the money, gave it to me and walked away with me holding the envelope and staring after her in disbelief. She said not a single word. I just gave the money to the trip organizer, and smiled thanking God.

Within the first year of my full-time ministry program, I was invited to speak at a camp put on by an international group called *Camp Farthest Out* (CFO). While at the camp I met a lady from Canada who was requesting special prayers. As she explained it, her husband back home was dying. He had nine terminal illnesses and was sent home from the hospital to spend his last few days of life. It was tough on her, so she came to the camp to receive spiritual strength so that she would be able to spend those days with him in peace. So, when she heard me speaking of how God was standing in there with you to comfort you in times of deep distress and pain, she just thought that I would be the ideal person to pray for her strength. Immediately the Lord started talking to me and said that I should pray for her husband's recovery instead. So, I asked her, "Would you like for your husband to be healed?" Obviously, she was not prepared for that, and was very doubtful in her response.

So, I took the initiative and started praying for her husband's healing, very simple, very direct. Her expression told me that she was not very impressed. And I looked her straight in her eyes and said, "Ma'am? The Lord said that whatever we ask Him for and believe in our hearts, He would give it to us. Now do you believe that the Lord can heal your husband?"
She waited for a moment and then said, "Yes!"
I then said, "Be it unto you according to your faith." She was trembling, and I asked her, "One favor though, when you get home can you please

let us know how he is doing?" At this, she was all choked up, and just nodded her head.

Less than two weeks later, I got a call from the person who invited me to the camp, saying that they had gotten a mail from the lady addressed to me. She did not know my address, so she sent it to the then camp director. In a nutshell, when she got home from the airport, she saw her husband gardening. He loved to garden. When she left for the camp two weeks ago, he could not even eat. He was being fed through tubes. He was supposed to be dead in another two or so weeks... but here he was moving about as if nothing was wrong with him. And yes, nothing was in fact wrong with him because he was completely healed of everything.

[HALLELUJAH!!!]

So, he offered that I should ask for anything that I wanted. Anything that I wanted, she would give it. For a season I was at a loss as to what I should ask for. Then I remembered that the next camp was going to be in the US. So, I simply said that I would love to be able to attend that camp. Her response was, "Just tell me how much it would cost and how I can get the money to you." The same weird tingling feeling I had when I realized that I would be going to school came over me once more.

Just two months to go, and I did not have a visa. And one of the worst news was that the US Embassy did not issue visas to people with convictions. Of all the problems I was being told that I would be facing, the visa was the worst; but funny enough, I was never worried about it. In filling out the form there were two questions that would always scare applicants: "How much money do you have in the bank?" and "Have you ever being convicted of a crime? If yes, describe it."

For the first one, I put exactly what I had in the bank— $3.45! It was amazing how almost everyone was showing me all the different ways to beat that, like forging bank statements and borrowing the money just to get the statement and then return it back to the owner. I was not comfortable at all with any of these. So, I decided to stick with my $3.45. There was nothing that I could do about the other obstacle— the conviction.

The day I went to the Embassy, I was nervous. Within about thirty minutes I was back out, without the visa. They turned me down. I then remembered that my "*Fairy Godmother*" had told me to call her when going to the Embassy. So, I called her that I went to the Embassy a while ago and that they turned me down. She said, "Stay right where you are and don't move. I'll call you right back". In about ten minutes my phone rang, and she said, "Go back into the Embassy, through the front door this time. Tell the security that you want to see the chief administrator of the Embassy next to the Ambassador. She is waiting for you. Give her your passport." I went back in, but the security refused to let me in to see her. People didn't just *walk* in to see people like that. So, I told him that she was expecting me. He reluctantly went to tell her about me outside. When he came back, he had a totally different expression on his face. She was right behind him and greeted me. She took my passport, and went back in with a *will-soon-be-back* parting glance. I took a seat and made myself comfortable. I watched all these people coming and going and gazing. I used the time to do some catching-up with the Lord about what was happening and how He was changing things up for me.

About twenty-minutes into waiting, the woman came out and handed me my passport and said, "Have a nice trip." She then went back to her office. Boy, was I nervous as I opened the passport— only to see the visa stamp staring at me.

- - -

The two years of full-time ministry was rough. The Church was not able to give me any support, but God was always sending something through someone. I was released from the Ministry a few months short of the two years and I was now on the job market. I started sending out application letters and nothing came of it. During this time I learned that God also moved through the working world. So, I started talking to Him about getting a job. It was during one of our talks that he reminded me that the college had a job placement department that helped past and present students make connections with the industry. The very next morning I went to the placement office and asked them if any placements were available. They said no. I hung around a while and I began to pray. Then, the Lord told me to go back to the office and tell them that a placement had come in but was not filed yet. It was still in the "*in-basket.*" When I went back and told them, it was as the Lord had said. But they were very curious as to how I knew, and I told them that the Lord told me. The manager of the department just burst out in praise. She was a Christian and was so full of joy when I told her that the Lord told me. And indisputably, the job was there at a very big industrial plant, and within two weeks I started working there.

On my first day at work, the maintenance Supervisor, the leading expert there on control systems, took a liking to me. He was an *Adventist,* and took me under his wings. Control Systems was my specialty and he showed me all the ins and outs of the system. He put pressure on me as if I was in class, and he even gave me assignments. After about five months, I ran into my old English lecturer from CAST. She came to my workplace to do business. She was the Director of HR at another big industrial plant. She was so impressed with my work and discipline at CAST and she asked me, "Don't you want a better job? What's your position here?"
"A *Grade-Three Electrician,*" I responded.

"You were trained to lead, not to work at the bottom," she said. I liked her way of thinking. "Come see me on Monday and I'll make you a *Senior Engineer*."

Wow! That's more like it. How could I pass that up? On Monday morning, bright and early, I was at her office. She put me through the basics of the paperwork and I started working the very next day as the Senior Engineer in charge of more than half of the plant, and a salary twice as much as I was getting. This was awesome. I was in a very unfamiliar territory now, but I learned fast. The things I learned from my mentor at the previous job came in very handy. No matter what type of equipment there was, the essence of the controls were all the same. The devices may have been different, but the connections and result were the same; using the three-phase principle from calculus: input, transfer function, and output. Once these areas could be identified, you were well on your way to a solution. That was the same basic engineering principle so I caught on quickly, and in no time was stripping down machines. In just over a year, I was promoted to *Senior Plant Engineer*. I was now reporting directly to the Managing Director. He was a very hands-on person and we worked well together at first. My task was to make whatever modifications to whichever machine as needed to make the plant more efficient. It was during this time I learned that the Lord was a *Master Electrical Engineer*. There were three old, abandoned machines, which the Boss challenged me to restore. Decades ago, the plant used to produce this product and had to stop because the machines broke down and could not be repaired.

My first step was to try and contact the manufacturer in England for any documentation or information that they might have had. Unfortunately, there was nothing since they had stopped manufacturing those machines decades ago, so they had gotten rid of everything about them. All I could do now was to dismantle them for inspection. To my surprise, I discovered that there were two ladies, still working there, that used to work on these machines. They had been there for over thirty years and knew about every piece of equipment in the plant. Their knowledge was invaluable, and they were more than willing to offer their assistance. We spent the rest of the week together as they taught me how these machines worked. I stripped them down to mere metal on the ground. And, based on my understanding of control systems and how the ladies described their operations I went on to design a new control system for them. I made up a list of electrical parts that I would be needing and gave it to my Boss. By this he was more than willing to give whatever I wanted/needed to make them work. Most importantly, he wanted to impress the Chairman, who was his father.

The Maintenance Mechanic volunteered and did the metallic cleanup for me, welding what needed welding. He straightened out all the cracks and bends. And by the time the electrical parts arrived I was ready. My boss imported everything, and in six months I had them up and running in semi-automatic mode. It took me about another three weeks to fine tune, adjust and calibrate them. The project took me approximately seven months, from start to finish. After doing all that work on the project and getting them to work in semi-automatic mode, all the Chairman could say was, "But they are not running automatically."
"But they were never able to run automatically, sir," I responded disappointedly. Obviously, he heard the disappointment in my voice and just walked away— and that hurt bad... *real* bad.

At that moment I decided that as soon as I got something else I would be gone. What was building up though was that my Boss had the attitude of a pig. He would curse "left, right, and center" and speak derogatorily to almost everyone and because of this, we were always in some form of argument or disagreement. Everyone was afraid of him and they could not express their displeasure over the way he spoke to them— that was not me. I told him straight up that I was not going to tolerate that kind of treatment. My telling him how I felt about his behavior did not do much good. After all, he was the boss, and he would talk to anyone in any way he wanted. But then, his father's reaction to me about the machines I had restored was the last straw.

At first, I was hesitant to leave because I felt obligated to the HR Director. The Lord must have been waiting for me to make a move, mentally, because two weeks later I got a call from the GM of a big processing plant. For three months, I let it just lie there. He called me again, "Just come and look at what we have, and you can decide." I still waited a couple of weeks while enduring my Boss's attitude. One day I just got up and went down to the plant which was just about five minutes down the road. He was excited to see me. He said, "You came right on time. We have a break down and the maintenance guys don't seem to be able to manage it. Can you have a look at it? Just look and give me your opinion." It was an industrial vacuum sealer. I had never seen anything like it before. And this was where Big Daddy showed up for me again. Within ten minutes of looking over it I saw the problem and showed it to him. And right there they changed the part, and the system was back online. "You did in ten minutes what we were not able to do in two days. Oh my goodness, you are much better than they say!" He threw his hands around me and walked me to his office. I felt bad for the maintenance team because he really made them look bad the way he said it.

In his office he wanted to know how much that was going to cost him. I simply said, "Nothing... When I was doing what I was doing I never thought that I was going to be paid, so it's on the house." The reality however, was that I did not have the slightest clue of what the going rate of stuff like that was and did not want to look stupid. In a sense, I was still a novice. So, what I thought was that I could use this as a bargaining chip– and I was indeed going to. During our discussion, I started pointing out the flaws, and hence the disadvantages I would be facing if I took the job. He agreed with everything I said, and it was obvious that he was still "green" at this thing, or they were very desperate to get someone of my caliber. I went straight to the meat of the matter, salary. I was getting a comfortable salary where I was. It was just the Boss and his abusive attitude. Mentally, I increased my current salary by 50% and told him.

I was preparing to start the real negotiation when he smiled and spoke, "No problem with that. As a matter of fact, I'll just round it up." And that nearly popped my eardrums. I never imagined that I would get that kind of salary. So, we agreed with a hand shake and set a date when I would return to sign the necessary paperwork. I would start working in two weeks.

When I handed in my resignation, my boss was a little shaken, but took it straight and said, "You can leave now and take the two weeks. I'll make sure you still get your full pay." I thanked him and wished him well. I went around to some other friends that I had made and wished them well too. A lot of them were surprised, but some of them said that they knew that I would not stay under those conditions. And they were right. In two weeks, I took up my mantle as a *Maintenance Manager* in my new job. When I started, I was greatly respected by the team because they had already seen what I could do and that I was no novice. That made my job very easy.

- - -

["*Whom the Son sets free is free indeed.*" (John 8:36)]

As I was walking on the street downtown, a car stopped in my path and two detectives got out and said, "Aha, Thirteen, we have you now! When did you escape from prison?" These police were one of the most dreaded officers in the force. One of them had killed more of my friends than I can remember. He was not one to be trifled with.

So, I just played it cool and answered, "I did not escape. I was pardoned." "No way! This could not have happened without us knowing. It would have been in the Force Orders," he said. He was clearly agitated and annoyed as to how something like this could have happened. And he was right. Under normal circumstances, when an inmate is being released after serving sentence this information would go to the Central Station and would be entered into the Force Orders. Every officer is required to read it every day when they come on duty. Also, if the released inmates had any outstanding issue with the law, then an entry would also be made in the Station Guard Logbook. In my case I was given an unconditional pardon. So, there wouldn't be an entry in any record there. They took me to the station for interrogation because I kept telling them that I was pardoned. The senior detective sent for the logbook saying that there must be something there with my name on it. To his disappointment, the officer came back with bad news. My name was not in the book. This irritated him. "Let me look at it myself. There must be something there!" He mumbled to himself and stormed out of the room to try finding something that didn't exist at all.

When he came back, visibly angry, I said to him, "Can I call my lawyer now?" That just rubbed salt into his wounds, and he practically chased me out of the station mumbling something I could not discern. Here again the Lord messed up the enemies plans for me. The Lord had set me free and here they were trying to imprison me again.

["O bless the Lord, o my soul, and all that is within me bless His Holy Name."]

- - -

After about one year on the new job, I found out that the company was reorganizing. They were about to close the Plant in Kingston and move the entire operation to *Savanna la Mar*, the location of the mother plant in Jamaica. I started to think that I made a mistake when I switched and accepted this job. "Did I do right, Lord?" I asked. The answer came by way of them offering me a senior position at the new plant if I was willing to relocate. They sure gave me a sweet deal. They gave me a second paycheck calling it a "relocation bonus." They would also take on the cost of moving my stuff to Savanna la Mar. And the sweetest was that they would find me a house and cover the rent. I couldn't believe it. The house was a big three bedroom in the nicest upscaled area of the town. I would be living two doors from my boss, the Maintenance Manager. This plant was about ten to twelve times the size of the one in Kingston.

I went down a few weeks ahead of my family and was settled by the time they came. It took some time to get settled in but we did it. I thought that this was going to be a big bonus in my life. A lot of money was coming in and no one could complain about anything, or so I thought. But, the next few years were the beginning of the darkest period of my life. Before I knew it, I was not talking to the Lord as regularly anymore; family life was on the decline and I started to struggle to keep it together. Sin had crept into my house and in a desperate effort to get things right, I resigned and moved back to Kingston with my family. We all tried to fit in at Grandma's house. But I was very uncomfortable. She did not like me from day-one. And to make matters worse it was taking a long time for me to get a job.

A friend of mine, who was an Elder at the Church I attended called one day, and said that his company needed a temporary building manager at their Downtown office. The current Manager had hurt himself and would be out of commission for a while. "You want it?" he inquired. "Of course, I want it!" I responded emphatically. The job came with a company car and an eight-man crew. As I settled in this new job my engineering training and experience kicked in. I never worked as a property manager before but at my level and the request emphasis I was given, I fitted right in. My primary focus was to find ways to reduce energy costs. I immediately took it on and hit the road running. My first month's report, even though I was not formally required to produce one, revealed that there was something seriously wrong with the light bills.

After doing my own investigation and audit of the system, I then invited the JPS (*Jamaica Public Service*) to send an engineer to verify our connection to them and to see if everything was fine. This they did and said that it was ok. I told the engineer, "I don't want you to tell me that it is ok. I want you to give me a report of what you did and what you saw. I sent you a request in writing, so I need your response in writing." To this he reluctantly agreed. I knew that this was what was going to happen. JPS would often treat their customers as if they were stupid, especially if you wore a tie and worked in an office. What I saw in the report was that JPS was making a huge mistake and was billing us wrongfully. I discovered that after analyzing all the billing information for the last two years. The figures were totally haphazard, and it was very clear when the error entered the system.

I submitted my full report and showed them that based on the bills and payments we were making we had overpaid JPS close to $4.5M. When the Financial Controller presented our case to JPS, they were livid and demanded a meeting and proof. You see, JPS absolutely would never refund money, and this amount? Hell no! But I did my job well and prepared a file for everyone on the Board, and it helped that I was going to be in the meeting. However, only my boss and his team got a copy of that faithful letter that was going to break JPS's back.

The Engineer that they sent to do the inspection gave us a clean bill of health as it related to our connection and operation and the interface between JPS and our Main input panel. So, after numerous debates and insinuations that something must have been faulty on our side of the distribution system, we produced the letter that was given to us by their own engineer, because I had called them in to do the inspection. I had done my own inspection before, but I needed the bill of health to be on their letterhead with their signature. And the room was silent. This was when I made my exit from the meeting. I was no longer needed, and my boss took it over from there.

The very next day I was summoned into the office. The company did not have an engineering department, and as you may remember I was only there temporarily. Right there they made me an offer to come on board to help them create an engineering department, and to head it up. Of course, I agreed. The company had over a hundred million square feet of office and executive apartment space, over a thousand tons of air conditioning systems, several standby generators, elevators in almost all the buildings and all of these must be managed by an engineer. Keeping the walls, floors, and windows clean was just aesthetics. The real work was with the equipment that no one sees, and this was where I came into the picture. I loved that job. I had two offices— which hardly saw me— and a team in which we made everything work.

The Engineering fraternity in Jamaica is very small and everyone knew everything about everybody; as such, one day I got a call from one of the biggest names in Negril. His family owned the largest number of rooms out west. He wanted me to come and look at his property because they needed a chief engineer. He said, "No commitment. Just come and spend the weekend with us and give us your opinion. You can go to Tinson Pen, and a plane will be there waiting for you." WOW! This was awesome. Even though I was slipping off, God never left me, and He set up this one again for me and I was treated like royalty.

The island was having a severe drought at the time and the underground tanks that serviced the hotel were down to about 15% and they would need about a hundred thousand gallons of water to service the property over the next few days. Negril— as a matter of fact, Westmoreland was one big watershed. I became aware of this having worked in Sav. I also knew a guy who had a couple of water trucks. Right away I contacted him and negotiated the provision of four loads of water, 450K gallons, to be delivered to the hotel, over the next twenty-four hours. The owner was standing right there next to me and heard everything. He even authorized the payments right there on the spot.

"You got the job. When do you want to start?" he said flippantly. I wasn't even sure he was serious. The way I simply fitted in and took charge of the crisis, even though I came all the way from Kingston impressed him. He didn't even bother to interview me. Before walking away, he said, "My secretary will set you up with a room for the weekend and you can start whenever you want. She will do the paperwork." WOW! I was to spend a weekend in one of the biggest all-inclusive hotels in Negril! This was when I started to get reckless; getting caught up in the *jet set* lifestyle. Not that I was living a random life, but I just was not paying attention to my relationship with the Lord any more like I used to. I was just doing my own thing. And it reflected in the instability of my family and the way I was conducting my life. And soon enough, this was the first time I was fired from a job.

The owner was a hands-on man; he and his wife, ran the place. I couldn't even remember the details of what happened, but I remembered that the owner and I ended up on opposite sides of an argument— and you simply don't do that with people like that. He even tried to besmirch me and the GM had to step in on my behalf. He was a bit of a vindictive person, and no one was going to get the better of him. This job was my largest paying so far. I had a personal apartment on the hotel property, a personal company-maintained car, plus I was given one of the hotel's executive houses. It was in a gated community where all the hotel executives who worked in Negril lived. It had some very beautiful four-bedroom houses, with all the perks: swimming pools, gym, laundromat, maids, the works. It was a good setup... but I messed it up. I lost sight of the fact that God was my mainstay. And it lasted only six months.

Being in Negril with my family in Spanish town was a disaster. It took a toll on my family life, not to mention the wear and tear it took on my driving the two hundred plus miles round-trip, which was done up to three times per week. On several occasions I would have to park under a random tree by the roadside to sleep in the car. When I moved back, my family was all messed up and we had to get counseling. I did not know how to maintain a family. I had no clue at all about the do's and don't's of family life. I never truly had one, and before I knew it the devil was wreaking havoc in and on my family.

When I moved back to the east, I was now spending my time trying to restore my family and this was where my inexperience showed up so conspicuously. I started to get very bored, and I think that I was falling into depression. But Glory to God; He stepped in and I started to get calls for consultancy services and it was putting food on the table. I was invited by the MD to this company to do a few inspections and a couple of weeks later I was offered the job as Maintenance Manager. This was a tremendous opportunity because it was very hard to get a job at this company. They treated their employees so well that the retention rate was one of the best. No one wanted to leave. No one was fired, nor did they want to go anywhere else. So, it was very hard to get in— and I was just called and offered this position. This company was huge, and the perks went along with it, fully maintained vehicle, and all.

This one lasted two years. I was laid off during one of the company's executive shuffles. I was well compensated though, and the money I got I used it to start a restaurant and a bar attached to it. I threw myself into this project with full force. My family at this point was now in shambles. The people that I thought I could depend on did not try to understand what was going on and decided to follow the cliché that the fault always lies at the feet of the man. And to some extent, they were right. If I had half the wisdom I have now, or was being counseled in like manner, I am sure that I would not have lost my family.

When I was growing up, the only thing I ever wanted was to have a family of my own. I was not interested in owning a house or car, wealth, land, or any of such possessions. I just wanted a family of my own. All I could hear in my head was, "*Daddy this*" or, "*Mommy that.*" And that left an emptiness inside of me. I *needed* to have my own family. I needed to come home to my kids, take them out to the park, take them on trips, and play with them in the backyard. I needed to come home to hear them screaming, "*Daddy, Daddy, Daddy...*"

I finally got it, but lost it. I allowed the enemy of my soul to sneak in and stole everything the Lord gave to me... and I was *furious*. So, this project was my outlet. A very nice three-bedroom house came with the property I had acquired for the business, but I gave it to the lady that was going to run the business for me. She assisted me in buying everything I needed to get it up and running. She was good, and had a very good knowledge of what was needed and how things should go. On the other hand, I was a total novice. I was not used to going to bars or restaurants. The bar was for "*pagans and rum heads,*" and restaurants were tabooed because I did not trust how the foods were being prepared, especially if they were cooked by women. Simply put, those were not for me, but as time passed, the business started to boom. Even while doing this, I was like a shell. I was grieving every day. I missed my family. I went through a litany of emotional trauma – anger,

VIVIAN TALBOT

hate, depression, loneliness. I was trying to figure out how I was going to get things sorted out. I gradually began to slip back into my former *"Lonestar"* life and was gradually withdrawing.

Looking back now, I realize that the time when you need God is the time the Devil gets you tied up in activities and business, preventing you from thinking about God. And you can get there so subtly without even realizing it. I was getting signs from the Lord, but business stole my attention away so often. This made the relationship I had with the Lord become just a shadow of what it used to be. I remained confident in God's Presence and I knew I needed to talk to and depend on Him. But, the "Best Friend" camaraderie was nothing near what it was or what it should have been. What made it worse for me to handle was the fact that I was so well-known. Not a day would pass without someone asking about my wife, and that was depressing. I wasn't handling it well at all; I didn't know how to. But I now realize that a major part of my inability to deal with it was due to pride. I was seen as this *"giant man of God,"* and was living a lie to maintain the facade. The other thing was that I was scared– yes scared– to open up to anyone at all. And with it too, I didn't quite know how to. I was always a loner; kept my feelings and thoughts to myself. I had been doing it for so long that I had now become an expert. I locked myself in a box. And every time I would do it God would somehow break it open and give me a refreshing view; but then someone would say something to me about how my wife (ex) and I looked so perfect together, and then right back I would go.

- - -

In reviewing everything, I now realize that the Devil had his eyes on me from the day my mother got pregnant with me. He somehow must had realized that the Lord had Big Plans for me and was trying to take me out. My mom spent the most part of her pregnancy in the hospital and at about six months they had to take me out. Being a premature baby I was left in the hospital for about another three months. I always seemed very sickly. I had countless escapades and near misses. But God had proven Himself to me and worked on my behalf. Because of this, I can now see that the Devil had been trying to take me out of the scene before I was even born. I know that I have a very specific purpose and mission in this life. And I am going to fulfill it, no matter what the enemy brings against me. It is only a pity, that I have wasted so much of my life over the years— but not anymore. But as they say, "Hindsight is 20 / 20." Things are going to change though. Unfortunately, we can't turn back the hands of time because we have only one shot at it. That is why we must align ourselves with the One who knows the route and possesses the roadmap of life.

- - -

After the business got under way, I had a lot of free time on my hands, and the thought of "Jaunts" came back. I was restless and came to Kingston and was employed as Plant Superintendent at a factory. That helped a bit until the GM and I had an argument over an issue. He did not like me because I was achieving what he was unable to do. He set me up, and I walked right into the trap. But in retrospect, I realized that it happened because I was not listening to the Lord as I used to, but should have. I lost the job as a result. God had always shown me things and guided me in paths that I could not see. He always protected me from unfavorable encounters and situations. So, losing touch with the Lord the way I did left me wide open to all manner of attacks from the Devil. Again, in hindsight, when I looked back on what and how things happened, it could have easily been avoided or I could have come out a winner.

This was when I started to buy into the idea of migrating, and putting some serious thought into it. Anyway, I started to hang out with an old school mate of mine. It was more because his mother was a teacher of mine, and he grew up to be a very prominent businessman in Kingston. He was glad to have me around, not because I was a prominent engineer, but because my reputation and influence was still strong and people (the wrong kind) still respected me. So, I hung around, gave whatever advice I could, and was paid for it. What was very uncomfortable for me though was that occasionally, I would find myself in the middle of a group or discussion that I knew that the Lord was not pleased with. As a matter of fact, my natural instincts would tell me that I should not be there. I didn't need the Lord to tell me that; I knew it. And if I did not get out fast enough, I would get swallowed up back in my past. And the Lord knew. No way did I want or would ever allow that to happen. God had brought me so far and out of a lot of things. So, I repented and decided to migrate.

The places overseas that I was acquainted with were not good choices; too many of my former acquaintances were there and that was what I wanted to get away from, my past. Sister Allison's son gave me an open invitation to come and stay with him until I got myself set up, anytime I needed. This was what I would do. So, I called and told him of my plans, and he was so happy to hear that I would be coming. It was then that he told me that he was afraid of me staying in Jamaica. So that was set. The next hurdle was figuring out what I was going to do with the business. Sell it? I didn't have the slightest clue as to what to do. But one thing I knew was that I did not want to leave the lady managing the business out in the cold. This was because if I sold it she would lose the house and would have to find somewhere else to live. I was the one who took her from where she used to live and work; I couldn't do that to her. So, I just signed over everything to her. "*Lock, stock, and barrel.*" Free of charge.

Thus, the rebuilding my life started; this was a strange thing to do in a new land and knowing only my friend. Then, God started to show me some very creative ways that I could survive. But I needed one very important thing– so, I put it to the Lord. One day when I was home alone, and my friend was at work, the phone rang. I picked it up, "Hello?" The person at the other end of the line asked of my friend. "He's not here," I responded. Then, there was silence on the phone. "Hello, are you there?" I inquired.

The lady responded with an amazing question, "Do you believe in God?" "Absolutely," I responded heartily.
"Do you believe that God speaks to people?" came her next question. My mind began to wonder what the Lord was up to now.
So, I answered, "Oh yes, I do."
The very next words just blew me away, "Well, the Lord just spoke to me that I should give you the car that I have parked at home. I just got it serviced, licensed, and insured. You can come pick it up anytime you want to."
"Thank you so much. The Lord bless you," I responded.
She replied, "You're welcome."

And the conversation ended as abruptly as it started. I stood there for quite some time with the phone in my hand in amazement and consternation. God had come through for me again. Not up to fifteen minutes ago I was just telling Him that I would need a car to move around in building this business I was trying to establish. And here, a total stranger gave me a car. I was still a little paranoid though, due to the reports one would hear about women in America and their *gift-giving*. So, when my friend came home, and I told him the story, he was glad for me and told me that she was a good person and was genuine. He said it was okay for me to accept the gift. After all, it was from the Lord, right? After about four days I still had not gone to pick it up. I needed to see how serious she was. Despite everything, and especially since I made so many mistakes in the past I just wanted to be sure and see how she would react.

A few days later she called me and asked, "What's wrong? Don't you want the car?"

"Yes, yes, I do want the car," struggling with my response, not wanting to lie, and at the same time not wanting to sound ungrateful, and too eager. So that evening I went and got it. It was a Volvo in peak condition; no strings attached. All the major jobs I had, offered me brand new cars as part of the remuneration package. Well, this was the first in a line of cars that the Lord had blessed me with that was not job-related. This reminded me— years ago a young man, during one of our prophetic training sessions, prophesied that I would get a lot of cars from up north (America). That was years before I was ever thinking about going to live in America.

When I thought of coming here, I was not thinking about a permanent status, but just enough time to at least get rid of the sour taste of losing my family. So when friends started trying to hook me up to get married, I was not having it. As a matter of fact, I was ready to avoid all hook ups. Mentally, I was not there yet— I was still grieving. And the notion of marrying someone who I was not in love with sounded sacrilegious. To me, it was an insult to the institution. But here, it seemed to be the name of the game; if you did not have a family member to file for you, then you had to find a woman who was willing to marry and sponsor you... for love or for money, literally. And there was no shortage of them around. There were a lot of lonely and desperate women who were willing, especially if you were from Jamaica.

In trying to see if I could get used to the idea, I accepted a date from one. She asked me, "Would you like to go to a banquet? My alma mater is having a banquet this weekend and we could go together." I responded in agreement. Unfortunately, I did not have any appropriate dress shirt, so I went to Macy's to get me one. I was working on a shoestring budget, so having to pay $75 for a shirt I really didn't need was a hard task. Nevertheless, I bought it, and once the weekend rolled around she came to pick me up and we were off to this banquet. Disappointingly, it was a dance and not a banquet as I thought. The people there were in the mood– except me, of course. I immediately knew that I was in the wrong place. When we went in, I was like a showpiece for her. Most of her friends came over to say hi, but, I knew that I was under inspection. What made matters worse was when they started to play the Soca songs and she invited me to the dance floor, which I naturally refused. But that did not stop her. She went on the floor and was *getting down*.

Due to the volume of the music in the ballroom, I started to have a terrible headache and was very uncomfortable. Obviously, she saw that I was not fitting in and asked me if I wanted to leave and I said "Yes." However, the thing that pissed me off the most was the fact that I wanted to go to Church in the morning and here I was at a dance. I felt dirty. It didn't seem to bother her when I told her of the fact that I wanted to go to Church in the morning.

"I am going to Church too. We do it all the time– go to party Saturday night and then go to church Sunday morning," was her nonchalant response.

By the time she dropped me off, I was so upset that I stormed out of the car without even saying goodnight. That was rude– I know. How could you invite me to a banquet which turned out to be a dance, and then say that it was ok to go to a dance than go to Church? I couldn't handle it. Going to Church was sacred to me. I know that was no excuse to be rude, and I never saw her again until about five years ago when we ran into each other at my Church office. In fact, she was the one who recognized me and reminded me that we even went on a date.

Anyway, life went on and I started meeting a few more ladies and this time one proposed to me. It took me a while to get used to the idea and we got married. Married? I was still hurting from the loss of my family back home. But I should have seen it coming; these women would pull out all the stops when they decide that they want you. Stupidly, I just went ahead without consulting the Lord. Not realizing that with that one agreement I was putting myself in a world of calamity. The signs were all there, but somehow, I ignored them. The first of them was that when she saw that I was reluctant at first, she was the one who suggested that we could get married and if I was not satisfied, we could easily get a divorce after two years, and that would be fine. The next thing, though simple, stood out to me; she was strongly against me getting a new pair of shoes for the wedding. She said that I should wear the old one I had. Why? I never knew. And I never did ask.

From day one, her bossiness came out. But, I took it in good grace. I just figured that I had to learn the culture of women in this new society. And like they often say, "Women rule." The real issue started when the immigration documents were to be signed and sent in. I was on my own. I had to find out everything for myself— what to do, where to go. Anyway, with the help of the Lord, I got the necessary information and got it in. When we were to go to the immigration office, she was reluctant and claimed that she could not get the time off. Again, I had to figure it out for myself and I went alone. The immigration officer was really upset with her for not coming with me and gave me a letter saying that she had better be there for the next appointment. Despite me putting myself in this situation, the Lord was standing right there with me. When she got the letter, she was less than thrilled. Our married life dragged on for the next few weeks until the next appointment, where it was obvious to the immigration officer that my wife was not enthusiastic about this. Nevertheless, I got my next appointment. This was when I would be getting the Green Card.

Everyday I found myself staring at the mailbox, waiting to get the appointment letter, but none ever came. Despite this, I knew the date because the immigration officer had said it when she had written up her notes. On the morning that we were supposed to go, she produced a letter that was addressed to me, saying that she saw it a few months ago but forgot to give it to me. When I took it, it was already open, yet she swore that she did not know what it was all about. How could she not? The envelope was obvious– it was from the immigration office. This was the day I was supposed to be going to get the Green Card, and I needed to be there with her. Again, she said that she was not able to come with me because it was too late for her to get the time off. She was pretending that she only just now knew the date. This was when I knew that I was going to need a whole lot of grace.

So, I said "Ok."

As the saying goes, "When yuh han inna lion mouth, tek time pull it out (*When your hand is in a lion's mouth, take your time to take it out*)." So, I played it cool. But she insisted that she would not be able to come with me, even though she knew that it would be impossible for me to get in through the gate alone. No single persons are allowed in; only couples. This was her way of controlling me. She wanted me to beg, and that was what I was *never* going to do, and I told her that. I was never afraid; just a little nervous, but not afraid. I remembered what the Lord told me, when I was in prison, "If I don't get to go through the gates I would be going up with Him."

That morning I had a good talk with Big Daddy and He told me to go ahead on my own. And that I did. When I arrived at the gate the gourd just opened it without any question at all. I was thinking that maybe he saw an angel or something. Anyway, I was in and waiting for my name to be called. And there it was, "*Vivian Talbot*," and I went to the desk. The immigration officer gave me a strange look and said, "where is your wife, Mr. Talbot?"

"She's at work, Ma'am. She couldn't get the time off," I responded nervously.

"Well, you cannot be here without your wife. And as such she is refusing to be your sponsor." She then took my file and threw it in the trash-bin beside her desk. She then turned to me and said, "You are now out of status and when you leave here you can be arrested and deported."

That was when my whole world collapsed. I had always heard of people being deported. Now here I was, walking right into it myself. Then the Lord spoke, "Do not move; do not get up."

"Wow, Big Daddy came to the rescue again!" And that's exactly what I did; I just sat there, the officer and myself looking at each other. For about five or ten minutes, we just sat there, not talking or anything; just looking at each other.

Then she made the first move. She hissed, pulled a desk drawer out and took out a single sheet of paper and put it in front of me. She pointed to four places to be filled out, and then asked, "Do you have $760, Mr. Talbot?"

"Yes Ma'am," I nervously answered.

"Go to the store across the road and buy a money order for $760. Mail it to this address. Do not look to the right or left, and when you get home do not leave the house until you receive the receipt in the mail. That receipt will represent your legal status," she instructed. I thanked her and hastily followed her instructions. I bought the money order, mailed it right there, went home, and stayed inside for the next four days. When my wife came home it was obvious that she was not expecting to see me. From the discussion that followed she knew that I would be deported. One of her statements was, "I don't want no immigration officer to come to my house. So, what are you going to do?"

It was then that I told her that I had to wait for a receipt to show my status. When I got that receipt, I hung on to it for dear life. This caused her to become extremely grumpy and dour in response everything. One day I asked her, "Why are you treating me with so much disrespect?" Her answer was, "Because you are too full of yourself! You act like you are so better than other people."

"Give me an instance," I challenged her.

Her answer knocked me out, "You don't bring your pay check home to me." When she saw the shock on my face she continued, "All my friends, who are married, their husbands give them their pay and the wives give them pocket money to take them for the week." Oh my God, I couldn't believe what I was hearing. This was the greatest insult to my manhood. Not even if I had working kids in the house would I require that of them to give me their pay checks. Wow! It was there and then I decided that I needed to get out of there. No matter the circumstances, I was not going to stay in this woman's house anymore. I did not know how to respond.

What I did next was, admittedly, a bit too outrageous to print– then I said, "I am all man. So don't ever treat me like I am a little girl!" She was shocked out of her wits and did not say another word, neither did I.

Later in the night she said, "Remember that you still have to sign the application in order for you to get the permanent Green Card."
"That's ok. The same God that allowed me to get the temporary Green Card, even when you wanted them to deport me, would work something out for me. If not, I have no problem going back to Jamaica. And as the saying goes, '*I did not throw stones behind me when I was leaving Jamaica.*'"

What I did not realize was that she had a secret weapon against me. The Card had already come in the mail and she had it and was hiding it. She was playing this close to her chest, and I never had a clue. But as they say, "Man a plan, God a wipe out (*As a man plans, God erases them*)."

After a year, I went back to the immigration office because I did not get the Temp Card as they said I would. And again, she was not there with me. It was then that they asked me for the temp Card, they sent me. "I did not get one," I replied.
"We sent one two weeks after you came here," they said.
"I don't know what happened. Maybe it got lost in the mail?" But yes, I did know. I realized that she snagged it. So, they gave me another temp card.

On my way home I was thinking to myself, "This is it." I was out of there. When she came home, again she was surprised to see me. "Surprise!" I said excitedly. Then, I simply said to her directly, "Where is the card?" Before she could deny it, I continued, "Did you know that it was a mandatory five years in prison for interfering and tampering with someone's mail?" That got her.

She walked away and went upstairs only to return a couple of minutes later with a government letter in her hand saying, "I saw this sometime ago and didn't know what it was." I took the letter and sure enough the card was in it. She was hoping that when I went there again without her or the temp card that it would be enough for them to deport me. What she didn't understand was that God took care of His Own, and Big Daddy was on the ball again. In a couple of weeks, I was out of there. I rented an apartment and moved in with one "pump up" bed (*air mattress*) on the floor. Three months before the expiry date on the temp card that I had, I applied for the removal of the temp status. They asked me why I was not living with my wife. I just told them the truth and within one month there it was in the mail; my permanent Green Card.

This was it. This was what everyone was killing themselves over. This little Green Card... that was not even Green. I endured so much stress and headache to get it, but God did it all for me. Despite all the lies, cheating, and conniving, My Big Daddy stood by me. I stepped out of His Will so many times but thank God for His grace and forgiveness and walking me through the fire and not letting me get burnt.

He truly brought me from the *Gutter-most* to the *Utter-most*.

ACKNOWLEDGMENT

There are so many people that allowed God to use them to bless me. I would need a whole book by itself to list them all. So, if you're reading this and you don't see your name here, please forgive me.

Rev. Dr. Sam Vassel, "*Pastor Sam*"; my Mentor. What can I say? We met while I was in prison, but you treated me more than a brother. You risked your life and freedom to assist me in so many ways. I can't forget when you encouraged me to study the Bible because in it was "*food.*" You did not just tell me that; you went ahead and registered me in the Bible study program at "*Source of Light.*" You took it even further by personally paying for all seven modules out of your pocket. For that I am *so* grateful. Your friendship went way beyond that we kept in touch and when I was released you invited me to your house for almost a full week and allowed me free access to your personal library which helped to significantly change my life. As a result, Bible study and a hunger for the Word and understanding it became my greatest love. Pastor Sam, what can I say? Bless you, bless you.

Sam Allison, "*Sammy Dread*"; son of my Spiritual Mother, *Sister Allison* "*Attita.*" Truly, and in every way, you are my brother. You have always been there for me. You accepted me when your mother brought me home to live, even though you knew of my background. You greeted and received me. We don't get to speak often, but when we do we catch up. You were really my shelter in a time of constant storms. You were there when I was lonely and depressed when I lost my family. You were there when I came to a foreign land and had nowhere to go. You put up with me until I could stand on my own two feet. I am sure that Attita is proud of you. Thank you for being my brother and friend in every sense of the word

Bishop Alvin Bailey. We became friends when you came with the group from *Bethune Avenue Holiness Christian Church.* Your messages were always strong and challenging, but what I remember most was the uncompromising and fearless way you related to us. Most Christians coming to Minister at the Gun Court were very timid and tried to be very "politically correct," but not you. You were direct and to the point.

Dawn Walker. Oh my goodness! You were the bravest of them all. During the review period everybody was trying, warders and prisoners alike. "Ms. Walker gwan like she nuh tek man" was the complaint of everyone, but she was very good at what she did. And as a result of the work done by her and *Blossom Dixon* a lot of guys got their cases reviewed and were either sent home or got their sentences reduced. Dawn and I became very good friends. I was one of the very few who was not trying to "pursue" her, and I think that played into why we got to be such good friends. She was the one who went ahead and made the connection between me and the *Myers, Fletcher & Gordon.*

Myers, Fletcher and Gordon, (Corporate Lawyers); through *Mrs. Dorothy Pine McClarty.* Ms. Mac was and still is my "*Fairy Godmother.*" She was the point person at the Office. The first time that I met her was about two years after they had taken me on as a project, sponsoring my education at C.A.S.T. without reservation. There was an immediate connection between us. One couldn't help but fall in love with this beautiful soul. And we immediately bonded. Even after I graduated and finished my two years of full-time Ministry, Ms. Mac was still looking out for me by recommending corporate individuals I should connect with. Through her I got to meet other very prominent lawyers and personnel in her firm. Special mention to, *Mr. Milton Samuda* who attended my graduation, *Mr. Derrick Jones,* and surely *Mrs. DaCosta* (she was so nice; Ms. Mac must have rubbed off on her).

Herbert Brown "Jungle Lion"; my first teacher at Gun Court before there was any school. He was my behind-the-scenes motivator and his influence and encouragement set the stage for the School and the Cultural program there. My poetry love came through him, and our wins at the highest level of the *Cultural Development Commission* in the annual drama competition was mainly due to his skills in writing and directing which he taught me.

Oku Onuoro; the creator of *"Dub Poetry"* was one of my favorite inspirations in the poetry world. I have heard of a lot of people trying to take credit for the creation of Dub Poetry but they all came after Oku. The first time the public heard it was at a concert put up by us at the Gun Court and attended by Oku. From that performance by Oku, Jungle and I put together twenty-five poems which became the foundation of the play *"Jamaica Struggle,"* which won the competition.

Bishop Robert McIntosh, "Pastor Bobby" of Maranatha Christian Church and the Maranatha family in Waterhouse, Savlamar and Karon Hall. We had a good time together having Church, prayer meetings, sharing in God's work, and our adventures when we attended the Conferences and Seminars overseas. I remember when we were having meetings at the Pegasus Hotel. The Lord moved us out and we spent quite a bit of time trying to acquire our own property. Then, the Lord directed us to the property in Waterhouse. Oh my goodness, the *miracle* of acquiring that property.

Kwame Dawes; a Literary Giant. You set the standard. My friend and I am inclined to reach out for the standard that you have set; a very difficult task indeed. Even in writing this book I crave your opinion and guidance in setting it forward.

Dr. Alfred Sangster and the administration staff of the *College of Art, Science, and Technology.* I want to say thank you for stepping up and helping me to set standards and make history. *Dr. Gossett Oliver* and the staff of the Engineering Department. *Mr. Gallimore*, one of my lecturers, thank you for the extra effort towards me.

UCCF '82 to '86; I want to shout out to *Fitzroy Vidal, Leonard Morgan, Elaine Williams-Morgan, Dave* "Mingo" *Hazel, Stephenson Samuels, Ricky HoSing, Oral* and *Sam McCook, Ye Kengale* (*Stephen Miller*), *Kevin Llewelyn, Stephen Mullings.* And the rest of the UCCF family from UWI and the Teachers' Colleges and Nursing Schools, please forgive me for forgetting your names (I forget names easily). The times we spent at our meetings and camps were very invaluable to me. And most of all I thank you guys for your friendship.

The Eternal Blessings of the Lord be on you all.

Forgive me for whatever and whomever I may have forgotten. I bless you all.

THE FAITH WALKERS' CREED

By FAITH
I will aggressively Pursue righteousness and be uncompromising in my rejection of sin.
If I stumble or fall, I will not be defeated but will arise and stand firm because...

By FAITH
I am a soldier of the Cross and shall live and not die.

By FAITH
The Word sustains me, and

By FAITH
The Spirit of God comforts me. Therefore...

By FAITH
Victory is my portion because I was born of a militant womb and

By FAITH
I am destined for a militant purpose.

www.ingramcontent.com/pod-product-compliance
Lightning Source LLC
Chambersburg PA
CBHW041630140626
46547CB00031B/1950